# Eating Disorders and Mindfulness

This book presents an overview of the latest psychological knowledge about the application of mindfulness-based interventions in the field of eating disorders. Increasingly, these interventions are used in therapeutic practice. They encourage clients to process their experience fully, as it arises, without judgement. Mindfulness-based approaches, in particular, emphasize the cultivation of moment to moment awareness of thoughts and feelings as well as bodily sensations. In so doing, eating disorders present an ideal context for the development of mindfulness. Indeed, it is in the body that the emotional and relational struggles of clients reveal themselves.

The authors in this diverse volume share a belief in the utility of using mindfulness-based practices to address disordered eating. It features up to date research and theory regarding mindfulness and the full spectrum of eating disorders, from Anorexia Nervosa and Bulimia Nervosa to Binge Eating Disorder. In addition, it explores how professionals can utilize mindfulness in their own practices, in the context of both individual and group treatment.

This book was originally published as a special issue of *Eating Disorders: the Journal of Treatment and Prevention*.

**Leah M. DeSole** is a psychologist in private practice in New York City, USA. She received her doctorate from Columbia University, USA, and has taught at Teachers College, Columbia University, USA and Hunter College, CUNY, USA. She is a member of the editorial board for *Eating Disorders: The Journal of Treatment and Prevention* and the author of *Making Contact: The Therapist's Guide to Conducting a Successful First Interview* (2006).

# Eating Disorders and Mindfulness
## Exploring Alternative Approaches to Treatment

*Edited by*
**Leah M. DeSole**

LONDON AND NEW YORK

First published 2013
by Routledge
2 Park Square, Milton Park, Abingdon, Oxon, OX14 4RN

Simultaneously published in the USA and Canada
by Routledge
711 Third Avenue, New York, NY 10017

*Routledge is an imprint of the Taylor & Francis Group, an informa business*

*British Library Cataloguing in Publication Data*
A catalogue record for this book is available from the British Library

ISBN13: 978-0-415-63457-1

Typeset in Garamond and Times New Roman
by Taylor & Francis Books

**Publisher's Note**
The publisher would like to make readers aware that the chapters in this book may be referred to as articles as they are identical to the articles published in the special issue. The publisher accepts responsibility for any inconsistencies that may have arisen in the course of preparing this volume for print.

MIX
Paper from
responsible sources
FSC® C004839

Printed and bound in Great Britain by
TJ International Ltd, Padstow, Cornwall

# Contents

# CONTENTS

# Citation Information

The following chapters were originally published in the *Eating Disorders: The Journal of Treatment and Prevention*, volume 19, issue 1 (January-February 2011). When citing this material, please use the original page numbering for each article, as follows:

# Notes on Contributors

**Susan Albers** is a clinical psychologist in private practice in Wooster, Ohio, USA.

**Robin Boudette** is a psychologist for Counseling and Psychological Services at Princeton University Health Services, Princeton, New Jersey, USA.

**Cynthia M. Bulik** is Distinguished Professor in the Department of Psychiatry at the University of North Carolina-Chapel Hill, USA.

**Christine M. Courbasson** is a clinician at the Eating Disorders and Addiction Clinic, Centre for Addiction and Mental Health at the University of Toronto, Ontario, Canada.

**Naomi Crafti** is a member of the Australian Psychological Society College of Counselling Psychology, Australia and works for FedUp? in Melbourne, Victoria, Australia.

**Leah M. DeSole** is a psychologist in private practice in New York City, USA.

**Laura Douglass** is Faculty Advisor for the Interdisciplinary Educational Studies Program at Lesley University, Cambridge, Massachusetts, USA.

**Rocío Guardiola Wanden-Berghe** is a member of the Departments of Community Nursing, Preventive Medicine, and Public Health and History of Science at the University of Alicante, Spain.

**Natasha S. Hepworth** is a psychologist in private practice in Melbourne, Victoria, Australia.

**Ann Knowles** is Associate Professor in the Faculty of Life and Social Sciences at Swinburne University of Technology, Hawthorn, Victoria, Australia.

**Krista Konrad Ingle** is psychologist at Duke University Medical Center, Durham, North Carolina, USA.

**Jean L. Kristeller** is Professor of Psychology and the Director of the Center for the Study of Health, Religion, and Spirituality at Indiana State University, Terre Haute, Indiana, USA.

**Rhonda M. Merwin** is Assistant Professor in the Department of Psychiatry and Behavioral Sciences at Duke University Medical Center, Durham, North Carolina, USA.

**Ashley A. Moskovich** is a graduate student in the Department of Psychology and Neuroscience at Duke University, Durham, North Carolina, USA.

**Yasunori Nishikawa** is a clinical psychology doctoral student in the Department of Psychology at the University of Toronto and University Health Network, Toronto, Ontario, Canada.

**Kathryn Proulx** is a psychiatric nurse at the University of Massachusetts, Amherst, Massachusetts, USA.

**Javier Sanz-Valero** is a member of the Departments of Community Nursing, Preventive Medicine, and Public Health and History of Science at the University of Alicante. He is also a member of the Department of Public Health, History of Science, and Gynaecology at Miguel Hernández University, Alicante, Spain.

**Leah B. Shapira** is Professor in the Department of Psychology at York University, Toronto, Ontario, Canada.

**C. Alix Timko** is Assistant Professor in the Department of Behavioral and Social Sciences at the University of the Sciences, Philadelphia, Pennsylvania, USA.

**Carmina Wanden-Berghe** is a researcher for the Department of Physiology, Pharmacology and Toxicology at the University Cardenal Herrera-CEU, Elche, Spain.

**Ruth Q. Wolever** is Director of Research and Director of Clinical Health Psychology as well as Assistant Professor in the Department of Psychiatry & Behavioral Sciences at Duke Integrative Medicine, Duke University School of Medicine, Durham, North Carolina, USA.

**Hannah Woolhouse** is a Research Officer for the Healthy Mothers Healthy Families Research Group, Murdoch Children's Research Institute at the Royal Children's Hospital, Parkville, Victoria, Australia.

**Nancy L. Zucker** is Assistant Professor for the Department of Psychiatry and Behavioral Sciences at Duke University Medical Center and for the Department of Psychology and Neuroscience at Duke University, Durham, North Carolina, USA.

# Introduction: Eating Disorders and Mindfulness

LEAH M. DESOLE

This Book of *Eating Disorders and Mindfulness* brings together some of the most significant research and theory regarding the investigation and application of mindfulness-based interventions in field of eating disorders to date. The idea for this Book originated from my experience working with patients who struggle with eating disorders as well as my personal involvement in the integration of mindfulness and psychology. My interest began over a decade ago when I was introduced to literature in the discipline of psychology proposing how the principles of Eastern philosophy could be integrated and infused within theories of Western psychology. Since then I have explored various ideas and means regarding how to enable people to live in the present, free from the emotional and physical suffering that often is attendant to simply being in the world.

In June 2010, I had the opportunity to attend a seven-day professional training in Mindfulness Based Stress Reduction (MBSR) in mind-body medicine taught by doctors Jon Kabat-Zinn and Saki F. Santorelli. It was an occasion for health care professionals from across the United States and around the world to survey the principle components and practical applications of mindfulness-based approaches to the prevention and treatment of a variety of physical and psychological disorders. The training was both exciting and eye-opening. For over 30 years, professionals at the Stress Reduction Clinic and the Center for Mindfulness in Medicine, Health Care, and Society at the University of Massachusetts Medical School have pioneered the integration of mindfulness into mainstream medicine and psychology through research, treatment and professional education. Since 1979, thousands of professionals have completed training in mindfulness-based medicine practices and tens of thousands of people have participated in MBSR courses. Participants in mindfulness-based approach have experienced marked improvement in both physical and psychological symptoms in addition to significant positive changes in health attitudes and behaviors. While at the conference, I met many mental healthcare professionals who work either with eating disordered patients or patients who are struggling with issues related to disordered eating. These encounters strengthened my resolve to bring this Book to fruition in order to encourage interest in the area and support the work of researchers and professionals who endeavor to bring mindfulness-based approaches to the field of eating disorders.

In contrast to Eastern culture, a divide between mind and body has been articulated in the West since the time of Descartes. Western psychology, however, now recognizes the intricate relationship between mind and body. Nowhere may this be more visible than it is in the field of eating disorders wherein Descartes' error, the fallacy of the dualist separation of mind and body or rationality and emotions, is "embodied" in those with whom we work. Indeed, the authors in this diverse issue share not only a common belief in the unity of emotion, reason and the body, but also a sense that mindfulness-based interventions are uniquely designed to address this unity and meet the distinctive needs of those who suffer from eating disorders.

Professionals in the field of eating disorders are continually seeking ways to enhance the provision of treatment and improve outcomes. To this end, there has been a paradigm shift in recent years from traditional therapy models to holistic, multidisciplinary models. Traditional therapy models, such as cognitive behavior therapy (CBT) and Interpersonal Psychotherapy (IPT), emphasize thought-driven analysis and verbal interpretation in their approach to treatment. In contrast, multidisciplinary models such as Acceptance and Commitment Therapy (ACT) and Mindfulness-Based Cognitive Therapy (MBCT) call attention to body based processes (i.e., the experience of emotions and physical sensations) within the context of the therapeutic relationship. These "third wave" therapies draw upon scientifically based research in developmental psychobiology and affective neuroscience to deepen our understanding of how the brain and the body come together in the development, manifestation and treatment of eating disorders.

Empirically validated mindfulness-based interventions have been applied in clinical settings for the relief of chronic pain as well as the promotion of effective emotional regulation for several decades. In contrast, mindfulness as it is applied to the prevention and treatment of eating disorders is in its nascent stage. Thus, the ten chapters included in this Book are investigatory in nature. They cover a range of eating disorders (Anorexia Nervosa, Bulimia Nervosa, and Binge Eating Disorder), treatment modalities (individual and group) and treatment settings (inpatient and outpatient). Although it may be operationalized in different ways, unifying these chapters is a common definition of mindfulness: meeting the present moment with full, *nonjudgmental* attention to one's thoughts, feelings, behavior and body.

To understand what mindfulness is, take a moment for this exercise. Stop. As you look at this page, notice the thoughts that arise in your mind. Perhaps you are thinking "How can they make an *entire* Book out of this subject?" Likewise, observe your feelings. Is annoyance brewing? Or are you feeling excited? Now try to discern *what is happening in your body.* Are your brows furrowed and is your jaw tightening or are the muscles of your face relaxed? What about the sensations in the rest of your body, e.g., your shoulders or stomach, can you describe them? Most importantly, can you go further and consider *the quality of your awareness* regarding your thoughts, feelings and physical sensations taken as a whole. What is the nature of it? For example, are you saying to yourself, "Oh, I ought to give this a chance. Why am I so skeptical?" A mindfulness-based approach would encourage you not to judge your awareness. Rather, you would be encouraged to notice it without evaluation; to meet your experience as a witness rather than a critic, in the same way that a researcher would observe an experiment.

How to make mindfulness meaningful *and* integrate it into the theory, research and treatment of eating disorders is the challenge of this Book.

The first five chapters in this collection are empirical in nature. The majority take as their focus mindfulness applications to group therapy treatments. We begin with a pilot study by Natasha Hepworth, "A Mindful Eating Group as an Adjunct to Individual

Treatment for Eating Disorders," in which participants with a range of eating disorder diagnoses participated in a short-term manualized, mindfulness-based treatment group as a complement to individual therapy. The next chapter by Kathryn Proulx, "Experiences Of Women with Bulimia Nervosa in a Mindfulness-Based Eating Disorder Treatment Group," examines the effectiveness of a mindfulness intervention not as an adjunct to treatment, but as a primary treatment modality. Subsequently, Hannah Woolhouse, Ann Knowles and Naomi Crafti investigate the effectiveness of a combined mindfulness and CBT group therapy program in "Adding Mindfulness to CBT Programs for Binge Eating: A Mixed-Methods Evaluation." This investigation continues with an chapter by Christine Courbasson, Yasunori Nishikawa and Leah Shapira. Their contribution, "Mindfulness-Action Based Cognitive Behavioural Therapy for Concurrent Binge Eating Disorders and Substance Use Disorders," also highlights the importance of acknowledging how eating disorders often do not occur alone, but rather present as comorbid concerns in treatment. This group of chapters concludes with "The Application Of Mindfulness To Eating Disorders Treatment: A Systematic Review" by Rocío Guardiola Wanden-Berghe, Javier Sanz-Valero, and Carmina Wanden-Berghe. Using a systematic review technique, the authors provide a preliminary review of research investigating the application of mindfulness to the treatment of eating disorders. They not only document the increase in interest in mindfulness in the field of eating disorders, but also find preliminary evidence of its efficacy in clinical practice.

The next three chapters are primarily qualitative, although some preliminary research data is presented. In the first chapter in this group, "Mindfulness-Based Eating Awareness Training for treating Binge Eating Disorder: The Conceptual Foundation," Jean Kristeller and Ruth Wolever outline the conceptual foundation and key components of a program they developed for the treatment of Binge Eating Disorder. In addition, they present current research and preliminary data regarding the efficacy of their program. Notably, the authors have developed a program that uses mindfulness as its foundation rather than an added technique. The second chapter in this section, "Psychological Inflexibility and Symptom Expression in Anorexia Nervosa," outlines an elaborate theoretical model of Anorexia Nervosa. Authors Rhonda Merwin, C. Alix Timko, Ashley Moskovich, Krista Konrad Ingle, Cynthia Bulik, and Nancy Zucker explore the ways in which mindfulness-based approaches may be utilized to address the particular concerns of individuals with anorexia nervosa, such as emotional regulation and distress intolerance. This section concludes with an chapter by Laura Douglass, "Thinking Through the Body: The Conceptualization of Yoga as Therapy for Individuals with Eating Disorders." In it, she insightfully grounds the mindfulness techniques of yoga in the disciplines of neuroscience and sociology as well as the philosophic underpinnings of yoga itself. She thoughtfully advocates for body based interventions and provides an explicit understanding of the inclusion of yoga in the treatment of individuals with eating disorders.

Also included are two feature chapters that are clinical in character. Two clinicians each write of their own experiences applying mindfulness to the treatment of eating disorders. First, Susan Albers describes the application of the principles of mindful eating to the short-term treatment of an individual with anorexia nervosa in a case study, "Using Mindful Eating to Treat Food Restriction." Finally, Robin Boudette writes in touching detail how her practice and study of mindfulness has changed the way that she works as a psychologist treating eating disorders in "Integrating Mindfulness into the Therapy Hour."

In the concluding chapter of this issue, Robin Boudette explicitly addresses the importance of therapists' developing their own capacity to be mindful *before* they take the step of applying mindfulness-based approaches themselves. Indeed, a general principle echoed by many of the authors in this issue is that doing this work is more complicated than it may appear on the surface. Moment to moment awareness of one's thoughts, feelings and sensations—without judgment—is no easy feat. Working consistently in this fashion with patients must come out of one's own extensive personal experience. Many agree that ultimately it is the strength of one's personal commitment to becoming mindful in everyday life that is the most important ingredient to applying mindfulness-based approaches in one's professional life. Thus, it is imperative that we prepare our minds *mindfully* to meet both the world and our patients if we are to respond authentically and skillfully to our patients' needs.

## Conclusion

Collectively, all the authors in this Book face a similar challenge: How to conceptualize and operationalize the practice of mindfulness into theory, research and practice within the specialized context of eating disorders. Researchers grapple with the practical, nuts-and-bolts aspects of how to not only concretize the notion of mindfulness, but also measure its effectiveness in treatment. Theorists wrestle to explore and explain the congruence between mindfulness and our knowledge of developmental psychobiology and affective neuroscience. And finally, practitioners search for the means to put knowledge into practice. One could argue that eating disorders present an ideal context for the application of mindfulness based approaches. After all, it is in their bodies that the emotional and relational struggles of our patients reveal themselves. Nonetheless, much work remains to be done. It is my hope that this issue will provide an impetus for continued innovation and exploration of mindfulness-based interventions in the field of eating disorders.

# Empirical Chapters

# A Mindful Eating Group as an Adjunct to Individual Treatment for Eating Disorders: A Pilot Study

NATASHA S. HEPWORTH

*Melbourne, Victoria, Australia*

*The objective of this study was to investigate potential benefits of a Mindful Eating Group as an adjunct to long-term treatment for a variety of eating disorders. Individuals (N = 33) attending treatment at an outpatient treatment facility participated in the 10-week intervention designed to enhance awareness around hunger and satiety cues. Disordered eating symptoms were assessed pre- and post-intervention using the EAT-26. Significant reductions were found on all subscales of the EAT-26 with large effect sizes. No significant differences were identified between eating disorder diagnoses. Results suggest potential benefits of an adjunct mindfulness group intervention when treating a variety of eating disorders. Limitations are discussed.*

With the growing popularity of mindfulness interventions, the application of mindfulness skills as a useful adjunct to ongoing treatment of eating disorders is of interest. Treatments for eating disorders, particularly bulimia nervosa and binge eating disorder, typically include cognitive behavioral therapy (CBT; Hay & Bacultchuk, 2001; Mitchell, Agras, & Wonderlich, 2007), Interpersonal therapy (Apple, 1999; Mitchell et al., 2007), and psychotropic medication (Hay & Baculthcuk, 2001; Walsh, Fairburn, Mickley, Sysko, & Parides, 2004). These interventions have demonstrated success in reducing disordered eating behaviors (Baer, Fischer, & Huss, 2006). Despite this, many participants do not benefit from these treatments (Kristeller, Baer, & Quillian-Wolever, 2006) and more recently the application of mindfulness interventions with people who have eating disorders has demonstrated promising results (Baer et al., 2006; Kristeller et al., 2006).

Mindfulness involves consciously bringing awareness to the present moment by focusing non-judgmentally on cognitions, emotions and physical sensations (Kabat-Zinn, 1994). Mindfulness is well suited to the eating disorder population because many sufferers experience difficulties with regulating emotional, cognitive, and physical experiences (Corstorphine, 2006). The majority of the research investigating the application of mindfulness to eating disorders has explored efficacy of the techniques as a stand-alone treatment, usually in a short-term format. An examination of the effect of a "Mindful Eating" group program that uses mindfulness principles as an adjunct to treatment for eating disorders would increase insight into the benefits of mindfulness in reducing eating disorder behaviors.

Research suggests that disordered eating behaviors may arise when individuals have difficulty regulating their emotional experience (Baer, Fischer & Huss, 2005). It has been demonstrated that individuals with eating problems frequently have difficulty tolerating negative affect and distress, and use food, whether in a restrictive or binge fashion, to regulate these internal experiences (Corstorphine, 2006). Individuals may then engage in experiential avoidance, defined as an unwillingness to experience negative thoughts, emotions, and physical sensations, and labeling these internal states as unacceptable and intolerable (Hayes, Wilson, Gifford, Follette, & Strosahl, 1996). According to this conceptualization, food restriction or overconsumption then becomes a short-term experiential avoidance technique (Linehan, 1993).

It has been proposed that excessive dieting and chronic binge eating, in an attempt to avoid these emotional experiences, often results in an inability to distinguish between hunger and satiety signals (Smith, Shelley, Leahigh, & Vanleit, 2006). Disordered eating behaviors interfere with an individual's capacity to recognize natural physiological cues related to hunger and fullness and also reduce ability to differentiate between these physiological signals and emotional distress (Pinaquy, Chabrol, Simon, Louvet, & Barbe, 2003). Furthermore, social conditioning to overeat or deny oneself food enhances physiological dysregulation and maintains disordered eating behavior (Lowe & Levine, 2005).

Based on the theory and empirical findings described above, mindfulness interventions aim to improve emotional regulation and enhance awareness of hunger and satiety cues by increasing awareness of internal states and reframing them as transient events (Kristeller & Hallett, 1999). Mindfulness skills assist individuals to increase awareness of emotional and physical states and respond to these experiences non-judgmentally without responding in an automatic and impulsive nature to alleviate negative affect (Kristeller et al., 2006). Furthermore, mindful eating techniques increase awareness of physical hunger and fullness signals allowing individuals to respond appropriately to hunger and satiety cues rather than binge eating or restricting food intake. For example, mindful breathing and body scanning techniques increase recognition of physiological hunger cues. Mindful eating also involves augmenting recognition of reactions and judgments about food, for example anxiety when eating chocolate, and helps illicit a greater understanding of food preferences and aversions (Baer et al., 2005).

Mindfulness based group interventions have been demonstrated to have a positive impact on reduction of binge eating frequency and increase sense of control over food (Kristeller et al., 2006). An exploration of a mindful meditation based intervention over 6 weeks in the treatment of binge eating disorder with 18 obese women found that ratings of control over eating and awareness of hunger and satiety signals improved significantly post-intervention (Kristeller & Hallet, 1999). The frequency and proportion of binging was also significantly reduced as intended. Similarly, an 8-week mindfulness-based stress reduction group found a small to moderate decrease in binge eating in 25 individuals with binge eating behaviors (Smith et al., 2006). Reductions in binge eating were attributed to improvements in self-acceptance and reduced anxiety symptoms.

Baer and colleagues (2005) applied mindfulness based cognitive therapy to ten women with binge eating behaviors and found a considerable reduction in binge eating and eating and food concerns, particularly the belief that eating results in loss of control of food intake. Other mindfulness interventions for binge eating disorder have demonstrated that improved awareness of satiety signals, but not hunger cues, was significantly correlated to a reduction in binge eating (Kristeller, Quillian-Wolever, & Sheets, in press). Finally, a recent qualitative study has also demonstrated that mindfulness-based interventions for eating disorders in six women with bulimia nervosa increased self-awareness and acceptance resulting in reduced emotional distress and increased capacity to regulate stress (Proulx, 2008).

Most research studies using mindfulness interventions for the treatment of eating disorders have examined brief group interventions independent of ongoing treatment. The primary group investigated has been individuals with bulimia nervosa and binge eating disorder. The current pilot study was exploratory in nature and aimed to investigate the potential benefits of a "Mindful Eating Group" using mindfulness techniques in reducing eating disorder behaviors for people with all types of eating disorders. Additionally, the study aimed to investigate the usefulness of a mindfulness group as an adjunct to longer-term treatment completed at a specialist clinic.

It was hypothesized that participation in the "Mindful Eating Group" would be associated with reduced dieting behaviors, oral control behaviors and preoccupation with food as measured by the three subscales of the Eating Attitudes Test–26 (EAT-26) (Garner, Olmstead, Bohr, & Garfinkel, 1982). In addition, it was hypothesized that individuals with bulimia would demonstrate greater reductions on all subscales of the EAT-26 than individuals with anorexia nervosa and eating disorder not otherwise specified (EDNOS) as mindfulness techniques are particularly effective with people with poor regulation of internal experiences typical of those with bulimia nervosa (Kristeller et al., 2006).

# METHOD

## Participants

Participants were 33 females (mean age = 21.42 years, $SD = 2.88$, range 18–30 years). All participants were currently completing longer-term treatment at a private clinic specializing in the treatment of eating disorders based in Melbourne, Australia. The longer-term treatment at the clinic incorporates regular sessions with both a psychologist and dietitian, and external medical monitoring by a medically trained professional. The primary treatment modalities used by practitioners in treatment are cognitive behavioral therapy and narrative therapy. Participants responded to an invitation sent by mail from the *Mindful Eating* program co-coordinators. The invitation outlined the structure of the program and indicated that the group was likely to be a useful adjunct to their ongoing treatment. Practitioners selected participants based on their level of progress in treatment including a BMI of 17 and above, self-reported improvement in mood and binging and purging behaviors less than once per day (e.g., once every couple of days). Participants were deemed unsuitable by practitioners to take part in the group if they were significantly underweight (BMI < 17) (as low weight impacts cognitive abilities) and if they were suffering from severe depression, assessed by their treating psychologist according to *DSM-IV* criteria (American Psychiatric Association, 2000). Invited participants were encouraged to discuss the program with their treating practitioners if needed. Participants were informed that a decision not to take part in the group had no bearing on their individual treatment or psychological and dietetic support at the clinic. Some participants did decline the invitation to participate in the group. The main reasons for declining the offer were the cost of the group, time restraints, and feeling uncomfortable about participating in a group program. Differences between participants who accepted and those who declined were not analysed.

Of participants, 30.3% suffered from bulimia nervosa, 10 participants, 51.5% from anorexia nervosa, 17 participants, and 18.2% from EDNOS, 6 participants. Diagnoses were assessed using *DSM-IV* criteria. The average length of time suffering from eating problems was 4.28 years ($SD = 1.96$) and the average length of treatment time was 11.12 months ($SD = 1.31$). The majority of participants reported experiencing current co-morbid psychological problems (63.7%), with depression being the most frequently cited (36.3%), followed by a combination of depression and anxiety (24.2%), and anxiety disorders (3.2%). Those with no co-morbid diagnoses comprised 36.3%. Of participants, 21 were students, 3 worked in the retail/hospitality industry, 3 were unemployed and the remaining 6 in various other professions. Anecdotally, participants were of Anglo-Saxon decent, however the race and ethnicity of the participants was ignored for the purposes of this study.

## Assessment Tools

*The Eating Attitudes Test*–26 (EAT-26; Garner et al., 1982) was administered to participants prior to commencement of the group and following group completion. The EAT-26 is comprised of three subscales: the Dieting subscale with 13 items relating to avoidance of fattening food and preoccupation with being thin; the Bulimia and Food Preoccupation subscale, with 6 items measuring thoughts about food, particularly cognitions representative of bulimia; and finally the Oral Control subscale with 7 items related to perceived pressure from external people to gain weight and self-control over eating. Although the EAT-26 cannot be used to diagnose an eating disorder, it is a widely used standardized measure to ascertain symptoms and behaviors characteristic of eating disorders in a variety of population groups (Ocker, Lam, Jensen, & Zhang, 2007). The EAT-26 has demonstrated sound reliability and validity in identifying individuals at risk of an eating disorder (Garner et al., 1982; Rosen, Silberg, & Gross, 1988). An EAT-26 score of 20 or higher indicates strong body image concerns and disordered eating behaviors, whereas a score of 19 or lower demonstrates low concerns regarding weight and food.

## Mindful Eating Group

The Mindful Eating Group is a 10-week manualized group program designed by practitioners at the clinic including dietitians and psychologists. The program was based on a mindfulness training workshop run by the Victorian Centre of Excellence in Eating Disorders (CEED). This workshop itself was adapted from Linehan's (1993) Dialectical Behavior Therapy using the mindfulness elements and modified for work with people with eating disorders. The Mindful Eating Group was also partially based on the work of Kausman (1998) which explores the myths of dieting, the concept of "non-hungry eating," and eating with awareness using nutrition knowledge and intuition cues. An outline of the program is provided in Table 1. Participants were also encouraged to practice mindfulness skills learnt throughout the program as homework tasks such as mindful breathing and noticing hunger and satiety signals, and using this to guide decisions about eating.

**TABLE 1** Mindful Eating Group Session Outline

| Session number | Session description |
| --- | --- |
| Session One | • Group set up and guidelines<br>• Introduction of the mindful eating concept outlining nutritional knowledge and intuition<br>• Mindful meditation |
| Session Two | • "Sharing journeys" of different food struggles and experiences<br>• Mindful meditation |
| Session Three | • Introduction of Mindfulness<br>• Mindfulness involves observing, describing, and participating in a non-judgmental manner<br>• Mindful meditation |
| Session Four | • Hunger rediscovery<br>• Hunger rediscovery meditation |
| Session Five | • Hunger and preferences<br>• Exploring food preferences and choices<br>• Mindful meditation |
| Session Six | • Guest speakers with past eating disorders and issues reflect on own experiences with mindful eating |
| Session Seven | • Barriers and obstacles to mindful eating and how to intervene<br>• Mindful meditation |
| Session Eight | • "Intervening mindfully"<br>• Identifying triggers and "hot spots"<br>• Applying mindfulness principles to combat triggers |
| Session Nine | • Exploring participants relationship with food<br>• Exploring how relationship with food developed<br>• Setting new food goals to develop a healthier relationship with food |
| Session Ten | • Practical and social eating<br>• Summary<br>• Post group EAT-26 completion and group evaluation |
| Session Eleven | • Feedback and celebrations |

## Procedure

Recruitment occurred at six different time points as there were six closed groups conducted over an 18-month period. Each group had between five and eight participants and a trained psychologist and dietitian conducted the groups. Given the pilot nature of the study and the limited availability of participants, individuals were assigned to the groups on a needs basis. While the proportion of each eating disorder diagnosis was not consistent between groups it was ensured that each group contained representation of each eating disorder diagnosis. Ten sessions were conducted over a 10-week period with a follow up meeting held approximately 2 weeks after the final session. The follow-up involved a meeting with group facilitators and each individual participant to verbally enquire about their progress and their application of the mindfulness skills learnt throughout the program in their lives.

## Data Analysis

The first hypothesis was tested using four paired samples t-tests to ascertain any significant differences between pre- and post-intervention scores on the entire EAT-26 measure and all three subscales. The eta squared calculation for t-tests was used to obtain the effect sizes of any significant differences identified. To interpret the eta squared value the following guidelines were used: .01 = small effect, .06 = moderate effect, .14 = large effect (Cohen, 1988). The second hypothesis was tested using a series of one-way between groups ANOVAs. These tests compared all change scores from pre- to post-intervention on the complete EAT-26 and individual subscales between people with anorexia, bulimia, and EDNOS. Differences between the six separate groups were not analyzed because of the small sample size of each group, and as such the inability to obtain statistically significant or relevant results.

## RESULTS

Comparison of pre- and post-intervention total EAT-26 scores indicated a statistically significant reduction in scores pre- to post-intervention (pre-treatment: $M = 33.46$, $SD = 14.80$; post-treatment: $M = 20.00$, $SD = 10.63$, $t(32) = 7.45$, $p < .000$). The eta squared statistic (.63) indicated a large effect size.

There was also a significant difference in EAT-26 scores on the diet subscale from pre-group scores ($M = 19.39$, $SD = 9.16$) to post-group completion ($M = 12.42$, $SD = 7.09$, $t(32) = 5.87$, $p < .000$). The eta squared statistic for this subscale was .52, indicating a large effect size. Similarly, there were significant differences between pre-group scores on the bulimia and food preoccupation subscale ($M = 8.52$, $SD = 4.20$) and post group scores on this subscale ($M = 4.70$, $SD = 2.69$, $t(32) = 6.55$, $p < .000$). A large effect size was identified, .57. Finally, a significant difference was also found in scores on the oral control subscale prior to group commencement ($M = 5.45$, $SD = 3.89$) and post-group scores ($M = 2.88$, $SD = 9.33$, $t(32) = 4.87$, $p < .000$). The effect size as identified by the eta squared statistic (.43) was also large.

The ANOVA conducted to explore the second hypothesis for the total EAT-26 found no statistically significant difference at the $p < .05$ level in change scores [$F(2, 28) = .29$, $p = .75$]. Furthermore, there were no statistically significant differences found in change scores between the three eating disorder diagnoses for the Diet subscale [$F(2, 28) = .15$, $p = .87$] or the Bulimia and Food Preoccupation subscale [$F(2, 28) = -.88$, $p = .43$] or the Oral Control Subscale [$F(2, 28) = .01$, $p = .98$]. Additionally, there were no significant differences in pre-group scores between eating disorder diagnoses.

# DISCUSSION

The present pilot study aimed to explore the potential benefits of a Mindful Eating Group Program using mindfulness skills as an adjunct to longer-term treatment for a variety of eating disorders at a private clinic. Results suggest a significant improvement with large effect sizes in EAT-26 scores following the Mindful Eating Group, consistent with the hypothesis. When exploring pre- and post-group change scores between eating disorder diagnoses, no statistically significant differences were found. These results did not support the hypothesis. The findings allude to the benefits of mindfulness skills in a group format as a potential useful additional component of ongoing individual treatment for people with varying eating disorder presentations and symptomatology. All findings should be interpreted as preliminary due to the absence of a control group.

Significant reductions in avoidance of foods and a desire to be thin as measured by the Diet subscale suggest that mindfulness skills can potentially enhance self-acceptance of one's body and appearance. Whilst self-acceptance was not directly measured in this study, it is encouraging that such a group program appears to elicit such changes. The ability of mindfulness skills to impact self-acceptance has been demonstrated in past research (Kristeller & Hallet, 1999). The post-group mean EAT-26 total score was 20 indicating the presence of body image disturbance and disordered eating behavior. The mean score indicates that although the program was able to reduce body dissatisfaction and problematic eating behaviors there were ongoing concerns. Given the chronic nature of eating disorders the findings suggest that ongoing, longer- term treatment is imperative in the treatment of eating disorders. Future research would be valuable to ascertain whether a mindful eating group brings about certain changes in specific behaviors such as a reduction in purging.

Past research also demonstrates that mindfulness based interventions reduce the actual number of binge episodes (Baer et al., 2005; Kristeller et al., 2005; Kristeller & Hallet, 1999; Smith et al., 2006). Although the current study did not measure actual reductions in binge eating episodes and compensatory behaviors, significant reductions in the Bulimia and Food Preoccupation subscale (measuring thoughts and actions typical of individuals with bulimic type behaviors) indicate that a Mindful Eating Group can potentially have a positive impact on reducing such obsessive cognitions and disordered eating traits consistent with the past research. Without a control group, it is difficult to ascertain the exact ability of a mindfulness group to produce such outcomes. Use of the EAT-26 as a primary measure for change, demonstrates the importance of including a test that investigates both internal changes in symptoms, such as cognitive patterns, and external symptom changes, such as binge eating. Past research indicates improvements to psychological well-being is perceived as a more pertinent indicator of recovery than actual reductions in binge eating behaviors (Hepworth & Paxton, submitted) highlighting the need to capture different constructs of change that occur in treatment.

Although not predicted, the finding that there were no significant differences in change scores between different eating disorder diagnoses was a novel result. The majority of past research that has explored the usefulness of mindfulness interventions in the treatment of eating disorders has focused primarily on bulimia and binge eating disorder (Baer et al., 2005; Kristeller et al., 2005; Kristeller & Hallet, 1999; Proulx, 2008). The current study demonstrates that mindfulness interventions can possibly be beneficial to individuals with anorexia nervosa, who are not severely underweight, and EDNOS, thus broadening the scope of such programs to include all eating disorder subtypes. Future research should investigate the benefits of a Mindful Eating Program in people with disordered eating behaviors who do not fit a *DSM-IV* diagnosis. Such people may include chronic dieters. It may also be of value to ascertain whether individuals would benefit from partaking in a Mindful Eating Group that is homogenous and therefore more specific to their needs.

Past research suggests that mindfulness interventions for eating disorders are effective in enhancing emotional regulation and decreasing anxiety symptoms (Baer et al., 2005; Smith et al., 2006). The current study focused primarily on improving recognition of hunger and satiety cues and mindfulness abilities around preferences and relearning relationships with food. A modified version of the current mindful eating group including an additional focus on affect regulation would be of interest for future research to determine the benefits of such a program.

There are a number of methodological implications to consider that suggest directions for future research. Firstly, and most importantly, there was no control group to clarify whether the improvements made were a result of the mindfulness intervention or other variables such as being part of longer-term treatment or due to normal improvement. Due to the pilot nature of this study, no control group or other means of comparison was used. A primary goal of the study was to demonstrate the potential positive effects mindfulness could have on treatment of all eating disorders diagnoses. As a consequence of this, further more detailed studies should be carried out in the future to quantify the extent of the positive impact of mindfulness over and above regular treatment options. Any suggestions or ideas drawn from the current pilot study are only preliminary. Future research should endeavor to compare the value of a mindful eating group to not only a control group but also a similar adjunct group using cognitive behavioral principles to compare efficacy. Secondly, the study did not include a follow-up to ascertain whether the improvements identified were sustained over time.

# REFERENCES

American Psychiatric Association. (2000). *Diagnostic and statistical manual of mental disorders* (4th ed., text rev.). Washington, DC: Author.

Apple, R. F. (1999). Interpersonal therapy for bulimia nervosa. *Psychotherapy in Practice, 55*, 715–725.

Baer, R. A., Fischer, S., & Huss, D. B. (2005). Mindfulness and acceptance in the treatment of disordered eating. *Journal of Rational-Emotive & Cognitive-Behavior Therapy, 23*, 281–300.

Cohen, J. (1988). *Statistical power analysis for the behavioral sciences*. Hillsdale, NJ: Erlbaum.

Corstorphine, E. (2006). Cognitive-emotional-behavioural therapy for eating disorders: Working with beliefs and emotions. *European Eating Disorders Review, 14*, 448–461.

Garner, D. M., Olmstead, M. P., Bohr, Y., & Garfinkel, P. E. (1982). The Eating Attitude Test: Psychometric features and clinical correlates. *Psychological Medicine, 12*, 871–878.

Hay, P. J., & Bacaltchuk, J. (2001). Bulimia nervosa. *British Medical Journal, 323*, 33–37.

Hayes, S. C., Wilson, K. G., Gifford, E. V., Follette, V. M., & Strosahl, K. (1996). Emotional avoidance and behavioural disorders: A functional dimensional approach to diagnosis and treatment. *Journal of Consulting and Clinical Psychology, 64*, 1152–1168.

Hepworth, N. S., & Paxton, S. J. (Submitted). Treatment perceptions in bulimia nervosa and binge eating disorder: A concept mapping approach.

Kabat-Zinn, J. (1994). *Wherever you go, there you are: Mindfulness meditation in everyday life*. New York, NY: Hyperion.

Kausman, R. (1998). *If not dieting, then what?* New South Wales, Australia: Allen & Unwin.

Kristeller, J. L., Baer, R. A., & Quillian-Wolever, R. (2006). Mindfulness-based approaches to eating disorders. In R. Baer (Ed.), *Mindfulness and acceptance-based interventions: Conceptualization, application, and empirical support* (pp. 75–89). San Diego, CA: Elsevier.

Kristeller, J. L., & Hallett, C. B. (1999). An exploratory study of a meditation-based intervention for binge eating disorder. *Journal of Health Psychology, 4*, 357–363.

Kristeller, J. L., Quillian-Wolever, R., & Sheets, V. (2005). Mindfulness-based eating awareness therapy (MB-EAT): A randomized trial with binge eating disorder. Manuscript in preparation.

Linehan, M. (1993). *Cognitive behavioral treatment of borderline personality disorders*. New York, NY: Guilford.

Lowe, M. R., & Levine, A. S. (2005). Eating motives and the controversy over dieting: Eating less than needed versus less than wanted. *Obesity Research, 13*, 797–806.

Mitchell, J. E., Agras, S., & Wonderlich, S. (2007). Treatment of bulimia nervosa: Where are we and where are we going? *International Journal of Eating Disorders, 40*, 95–101.

Ocker, L. B., Lam, E. T. C., Jensen, B. E., & Zhang, J. J. (2007). Psychometric properties of the Eating Attitudes Test. *Measurement in Physical Education and Exercise Science, 11*, 25–48.

Pinaquy, S., Chabrol, H., Simon, C., Louvet, J. P., & Barbe, P. (2003). Emotional eating, alexithymia, and binge-eating disorder in obese women. *Obesity Research, 11*, 195–201.

Proulx, K. (2008). Experiences of women with bulimia nervosa in a mindfulness-based eating disorder treatment group. *Eating Disorders: The Journal of Treatment and Prevention, 16*, 52–57.

Rosen, J., Silberg, N. T., & Gross, J. (1988). Eating Attitudes Test and eating disorders Inventory: Norms for adolescent girls and boys. *Journal of Consulting and Clinical Psychology, 56*, 305–308.

Smith, B. W., Shelley, B. M., Leahigh, L., & Vanleit, B. (2006). A preliminary study of the effects of a modified mindfulness intervention on binge eating. *Complementary Health Practice Review, 11*, 133–143.

Walsh, B. T., Fairburn, C. G., Mickley, D., Sysko, R., & Parides, M. K. (2004). Treatment of bulimia nervosa in a primary care setting. *American Journal of Psychiatry, 161*, 556–561.

# Experiences of Women with Bulimia Nervosa in a Mindfulness-Based Eating Disorder Treatment Group

KATHRYN PROULX

*University of Massachusetts, Amherst, Massachusetts, USA*

*The experience of 6 college-age women with bulimia nervosa was examined after they participated in an 8-week mindfulness-based eating disorder treatment group. This phenomenological study used individual interview and pre- and post-treatment self-portraits. Participants described their experience of transformation from emotional and behavioral extremes, disembodiment, and self-loathing to the cultivation of an inner connection with themselves resulting in greater self-awareness, acceptance, and compassion. They reported less emotional distress and improved abilities to manage stress. This treatment may help the 40% of women who do not improve with current therapies and might be useful to prevent symptoms in younger women.*

In response to the cultural idealization of thinness, over 50% of adolescent girls think they are overweight and consequently diet (Fisher et al., 1995). Moreover, 5 to 10 million adolescent girls and women in the United States are estimated to struggle with eating disorders (National Eating Disorders Association, 2006). Bulimia nervosa occurs in 1 to 4% of American college-age women (American Psychiatric Association [APA], 2000).

An episode of binge eating is characterized by eating, within a two-hour period of time, an amount of food that is definitely larger than most people would eat during a similar period of time in similar circumstances (APA, 2000). Individuals with bulimia nervosa experience a sense of lack of control over their eating during the episode including the feeling either that one cannot stop eating, control how much one is eating, or control the type of foods eaten. Recurrent inappropriate compensatory behaviors include self-induced vomiting, the misuse of laxatives, diuretics, diet pills, medications, fasting, and excessive exercise. Individuals with bulimia nervosa are often normal weight or overweight, making it a hidden disorder.

Bulimia nervosa typically begins with a fear of weight gain and the need for dieting (Fairburn & Cooper, 1982; Pipher, 1994). Self-imposed starvation eventually leads to binge eating in 30–50% of patients with anorexia nervosa referred for treatment (Garfinkel, Moldofsky, & Garner, 1980; Hsu, Crisp, & Harding, 1979). The gradual breakdown of self-control and the emergence of binge eating typically occur about nine months after the initiation of dieting (Garfinkel, Moldofsky, & Garner, 1980).

Gradually, the eating binges get separated from mealtime or desire for food and become more and more a response to emotional upset. Once bulimia is entrenched, it functions to reduce stress and is triggered by such emotions as anxiety, anger, and depression. Over time, the behavior takes on a life of its own where eventually pleasure and normal interpersonal relationships are replaced by compulsion, secrecy, and guilt. According to Bruch (1988), the drive for excessive thinness experienced by young women with bulimia nervosa acts as a "cage" that constricts their psychological growth and the development of a genuine self.

Many college-age women with bulimia nervosa are disconnected from their bodies and feelings, rendering them easily influenced by cultural pressures and peer expectations (Brown & Gilligan, 1992; Pipher, 1994). These women experience low self-esteem, anxiety, depression, and interpersonal difficulties (Bruch, 1988). Without treatment, bulimia nervosa readily progresses to a chronic illness with deleterious medical, psychological, and social outcomes. For those women with bulimia nervosa who receive treatment, up to 40% are resistant to current known treatment interventions including cognitive behavioral treatment (CBT), medications, and interpersonal psychotherapy (Fairburn, Agras, & Wilson, 1992; Stice, 1999).

MBSR is a systems-based, self-regulation practice that focuses attention on the present moment without judgment and with self-compassion (Kabat-Zinn, 1990, 1994). By raising nonjudgmental awareness of the individual's experience in the moment, space is created around experience to cognitively label what is happening thereby reducing automatic emotional reactivity (Bennett-Goleman, 2001). The practice includes formal and informal meditation, which help to cultivate a state of relaxation, connection with the body, innate wisdom, and personal insight (Hanh, 1975).

Because women with bulimia nervosa tend to struggle with issues of perfection, control, and extremely harsh self-criticism (Bruch, 1988; Richards, Hardman, & Berrett, 2007), the gentle, compassionate intention behind MBSR offers an alternative lifestyle approach that becomes a lifelong practice unique to each person. It potentially impacts issues related to self-awareness (Mason & Hargreaves, 2001), identity (Santorelli, 1992), affect regulation (Dalai Lama & Goleman, 2003), depression (Segal, Williams, &

Teasdale, 2002), anxiety (Kabat–Zinn et al., 1992; Miller, Fletcher, & Kabat-Zinn, 1995), self-esteem (Roth & Creaser, 1997), interpersonal effectiveness (Shapiro, Schwartz, & Bonner, 1998), coping and problem solving (Segal, Williams, & Teasdale, 2002), impulse control (Kristeller & Hallett, 1999), and compassion (Shapiro, Schwartz, & Bonner, 1998) all of which form the hypothesized roots of bulimia nervosa. In addition, since MBSR is offered as a group treatment modality, there is the added benefit of social support to enhance participants' problem solving abilities, coping skills, and interpersonal communication.

The purpose of this study was to understand how college-age women with bulimia nervosa experience participation in the self-regulatory intervention of the M-BED group. Since the onset of bulimia nervosa frequently occurs in college-age women, effective treatment programs available within a college mental health setting could prevent its progression to a chronic disorder. If the M-BED group was effective in diminishing underlying core psychological and developmental issues contributing to the development of eating disorders such as bulimia nervosa, it is possible that, MBSR offered to young women earlier in their psychosocial development, might assist in the prevention of eating disorders.

# METHODS

A phenomenological design was chosen by the researcher to deepen understanding of the participants' experience of the M-BED group. The philosophy of phenomenology (Husserl, 1913/1983) is highly congruent with mindfulness practice (Depraz, Varela, & Vermesch, 2003).

## Sample and Setting

Six college-age women with bulimia nervosa were purposively sampled to participate in this phenomenological study. Participants were recruited via referrals from the mental health centers of a five-college consortium and local psychotherapists. All six women who participated in the M-BED group had been diagnosed with bulimia nervosa according to criteria explicated in the DSM-IV-TR (APA, 2000). All participants had experienced eating disorder symptoms for many years. Participants were engaged in individual psychotherapy so that if challenging psychological issues arose as defenses were lowered by meditation, there was an ongoing source of emotional support. Given that bingeing, purging, and over-exercising can threaten the health of women with bulimia nervosa, participants each had a recent physical examination and maintained an ongoing relationship with a primary care provider. The women in the study did experience comorbid mood or anxiety disorders and some were taking psychotropic medications. None of the participants met DSM-IV-TR criteria for substance abuse or Dissociative

Identity Disorder. Participants had access to 24-hour emergency medical and psychological services.

## Procedure

The researcher met with each woman referred to the study to review specific information about the M-BED group, the requirements for participation in the study, and to obtain written informed consent. During this initial interview, demographic data, information about prior meditation experience, and a full psychiatric history was completed. Participants also created a self-portrait using the art medium of their choice.

## Mindfulness-Based Eating Disorder Treatment Group (M-BED Group)

The M-BED group members participated in eight, 2-hour sessions led by the researcher. Each session contained 4 components: experiential meditation practice, psychoeducation, discussion and assigned home practice. For home practice, participants used researcher-created CDs to guide a 10- or 30-minute body scan or sitting meditation. Handouts reinforced the psychoeducational component of each session (Table 1).

## Post-Group Interview

After the M-BED group treatment, participants were interviewed one on one to understand their lived experience of the group. The audiotaped interview began with a general question aimed at understanding which parts of the M-BED group were helpful, unhelpful, or stressful. Since core issues of women with bulimia nervosa include disconnection from their feelings and bodies with difficulty regulating their emotions and controlling their impulses, I was interested in understanding how participating in the M-BED group affected the women's self-awareness, affect regulation, and impulse-control. Few studies have examined the concept of intentionality, a concept central to MBSR and phenomenology (Proulx, 2003). Therefore I explored how the participants experienced the mindful intentions of nonjudgment, self-compassion, loving kindness, and acceptance during and after the M-BED group. Since the mechanism of action underlying MBSR has not been determined (Bishop, 2002; Proulx, 2003), I wanted to understand how the women in the M-BED group experienced both the formal and informal mindfulness meditation practices. To explore how participation in the M-BED group impacted the women's relationships with their bodies, they were asked to create a self-portrait using the art medium of their choice and to describe their impressions of their initial and final self-portraits separately and in relation to one another.

**TABLE 1** Session Outlines

| Session | Discussion | Psychoeducation | Experiential | Home Practice |
|---------|------------|-----------------|--------------|---------------|
| | | Component | | |
| 1 | Introduction. Q & A after meditation | Overview of MBSR | Raison eating exercise, diaphragmatic breathing body scan | Daily body scan using CD. Complete Pleasant Events calendar. Eat one meal mindfully over the week. Journaling. |
| 2 | Review home practice. Discuss pleasant events noticed, discuss experience and impact of stress, begin list of stress triggers. | Mind-body connection, stress-reaction cycle, effects of emotional reactivity, differences between reacting and responding to stress | Body scan, sitting meditation, mini-meditation | Daily formal meditation using CD. Eat 2 meals mindfully over the week. Mini-meditation before eating and throughout day. Notice triggers of stress and emotional reactivity. Complete Unpleasant Events calendar. Journaling. |
| 3 | Review home practice. Discuss the Unpleasant Events Calendars, triggers of and common reactions to stress. Generated a list of self-soothing and coping strategies using examples from participants' experiences. | The value of self-awareness in recognizing triggers of stress that lead to binging and purging. Strategies for coping with and lowering stress as alternatives to binging, purging, or self-harming behaviors. | Yoga | Daily formal meditation using CD. Eat three meals mindfully over the week Continued practice of mini-meditation before eating and at intervals throughout the day. Continue to notice triggers of stress and the impact of stress on their bodies. Begin using a list of self-soothing strategies to lower and cope with stress. Journaling. |

| | | | |
|---|---|---|---|
| 4 | Review home practice. What was noticed about their triggers of stress, where they felt stress in their bodies, and ways they coped. Participants discussed their thought patterns, self-judgment, constant comparison to others, control issues, and perfectionism. | The mindful intentions of nonjudgment, loving kindness, compassion, acceptance, and patience were introduced as alternative way of being and relating to oneself. | Loving-kindness meditation with positive self-touch | Daily formal meditation practice using CD. Eat four meals mindfully over the course of the week. Use mini-meditation before eating and throughout day. Become increasingly aware of the tendencies towards judgment, control and perfectionism. Alternatively, practice the mindful qualities of nonjudgment, loving kindness, compassion, acceptance, and patience in their day-to-day lives. Journaling |
| 5 | Review home practice. Patterns in the women's tendencies towards self-judgment, control, perfection-ism, and comparison to others were shared. Their experiences with the mindful intentions of nonjudgment, loving-kindness, compassion, acceptance, and patience during the previous week were discussed. They shared the ways their families impacted their sense of self, either as a source of stress or support and whether they were able to be authentic in their family relationships. | Relationships with family and friends impact our sense of identity, self worth, and level of stress. | Sitting meditation | Daily formal meditation practice using CD. Eat 5 meals mindfully over the week. Continue with mini-meditation before meals and throughout the day. Notice how relationships impacted their sense of self and whether their relationships were a source of support or stress. When aware of stress, practice nonjudgment, compassion and self-soothing strategies. Journaling |
| 6 | Review home practice. Discussed issues of trust and getting their needs met within their interpersonal relationships. Discussed their eating patterns, the quality of their binging and purging behaviors, triggers of binges, and the range of emotional needs underlying the binge eating. | The concept of hunger and taste satiety was presented. Styles of communication were presented and handouts summarizing the advantages and disadvantages of each style were provided. | Eating Exercises: Awareness of HungerAwareness of FullnessTaste Satiety | Daily formal meditation practice using CD. Eat 6 meals mindfully over the week, noticing degree of hunger, fullness and taste satiety. Continue with mini-meditation before meals and throughout day. Notice patterns of communication styles in their relationships and the thoughts and feelings associated with these styles. Journaling. |

*(Continued)*

**TABLE 1** (Continued)

| | | Component | | |
|---|---|---|---|---|
| Session | Discussion | Psychoeducation | Experiential | Home Practice |
| 7 | Experiences with assertive, aggressive, and passive communications styles were discussed. The participants shared their thoughts and feelings related to hunger and satiety over the previous week. A meal to be eaten in the final group was planned. Reactions to Slim Hopes documentary. | Viewed the Media Education Foundation documentary, Slim Hopes (Jhally & Kilbourne, 1995). | Walking meditation | Daily formal meditation practice using the CD. Eat 7 meals mindfully over the week using the mini-meditation before meals and as needed to raise self-awareness and lower anxiety. As they occur throughout their day, notice the impact of media images and cultural pressures on their values and sense of identity. Journaling. |
| 8 | Group members reviewed their observations of media and cultural messages over the previous week and how these impacted their sense of self, body image, and authenticity. The book, *One Size Does Not Fit All* (Naidus, 1993) was passed among all the participants. Each women selected pages from the book with which they resonated and shared with one another what the images evoked for them. Frank sharing about the compulsive and secretive nature of their disorder spontaneously arose. | Aspects of a healthy lifestyle were presented synthesizing the components learned throughout the prior seven weeks of the M-BED group. Ways to continue their mindfulness practice after the M-BED group. | Participants ate a dinner of salad and burritos together throughout the group. Wisdom meditation. | A list of further readings on MBSR was provided as well as the contact information for several area sanghas or meditation centers. |

## Data Analysis

To arrive at a deeper understanding of the participants' experience of the M-BED group, data analysis was completed from a phenomenological, interpretive hermeneutic perspective. Data analysis began with identifying and bracketing (Husserl, 1913/1983; van Manen, 1990) my own preconceived beliefs, assumptions, and values related to the M-BED group. As such my process of mindful self-reflection began before the study and continued throughout every aspect of the study including recruitment of participants, data collection, data analysis, and the phenomenological writing process. This practice cultivates a deeper, authentic self-understanding.

### IDENTIFYING THEMES

To gain a thorough understanding of the participants' experience in the M-BED group, all of the data collected in the study were carefully read using a combination of the wholistic reading approach, the selective reading approach, and the detailed reading approach outlined by van Manen (1990, pp. 92–96). Once the data was closely examined and highlighted, themes were identified in the margins of the transcripts.

### CREATING A SYNTHESIS OF INTENTIONALITY

According to Drew (2001, 2004), the phenomenon that is explored in a phenomenological study originates from the researcher's consciousness and intentionality toward the empirical world. Because the impetus for the research, selection of the topic, and the final description come from the researcher, researcher self-awareness of that intentionality is crucial to the study's validity (Drew, 1999, 2001, 2004; Fleming, Gaidys, & Robb, 2003). Following Drew's (2001, 2004) guidelines, the researcher first developed a phenomenology of her personal experience in order to identify and understand her relationship with the research phenomenon. Next, following an eight step process, a synthesis of intentionality was created that represented both the researcher's and the participants' experience of the M-BED group, reconstituting the phenomenon into a whole.

## RESULTS

Analysis of the interview transcripts, journals, self portraits and the researcher's experience was organized into five main themes: (1) sense of self before the group, (2) coping strategies before the group, (3) connection with one another in the M-BED group, (4) connection with themselves through meditation, and (5) shifts in relationship to self and others resulting in new coping strategies at the conclusion of the M-BED group. The results presented below will include personal narrative and self-portrait data. The names of the six participants: Ana, Kelley, Rena, Sophia, Eva, and Ruth as they appear below are fictitious to preserve their confidentiality.

## Participants' Sense of Self before the M-BED Group

At the beginning of this study, the women in the M-BED group reported experiencing extremes in their thoughts, feelings, and behavior. They felt worthless, unlovable, inadequate, powerless, victimized, angry, sad, and numb. In an effort to feel lovable they engaged in a driven pursuit of external achievements, abusive or sexualized relationships, and culturally defined beauty. Rena explains that "I was focused on being thin, pretty, and perfect in order to attract the prince who would provide me with love so I would be happy evermore" (Figure 1).

All of the women were out of touch with their authentic selves, their bodies, and their personal needs. The following statements by the participants illustrate the nature of their relationship to their bodies. Kelley was so disembodied she admits, "I actually took pictures of myself without my head because I didn't want to know that it was me. When I look into a mirror I simply say to myself, 'that isn't me.'" Rena confides, "Prior to the M-BED group I often "just wanted to get a knife and cut off my abdomen, I hated it so much." Ruth describes her objectified stomach this way, "I'd think about my stomach as another unit, a thing, not a part of me." More globally Ana remarked, "I guess I don't recognize my body as being important or valid."

The women could not trust themselves or others to meet their needs because their needs were perceived as being either too great or altogether unimportant. Sophia shared the following about her relationships, "I feel like I approach every social interaction loaded with all kinds of ideas of who I think I am, or how I ought to act, or what this person wants form me, to the point that it interferes with my being able to focus on what they're saying. I feel like I have to assume a certain personality for the person I am talking with, which makes it hard for me to have social conversations with people because I have so much performance anxiety. When I am in a room with a bunch of people they envelop me instead of me being able to stay grounded in myself. I don't feel a core self."

Because of their disconnection from their inner selves and their underlying, negative beliefs about themselves, the women experienced great difficulty regulating their extreme feelings, causing their behaviors to become out of control. Based on their temperaments, family experiences, and cultural expectations, they developed a belief system that if they achieved the perfect body size and shape, they would be seen as successful and loveable.

**FIGURE 1** Rena's Pre-Group Self Portrait.

## Participants' Coping Strategies Before the M-BED Group

In response to this belief system, they adopted the coping behaviors of restricting eating, which then progressed to bingeing and purging. The women's thoughts, feelings, and behaviors were aimed at control, self-sufficiency, and completeness in response to their internal sense of lack of control, dependency, and incompleteness. They had grown to hate their personal experience of vulnerability and human need, closing off to authentic relational life with self and other.

When controlling food and purging activities were insufficient or unavailable, many of the women resorted to cutting themselves to obtain relief from their excruciating feelings and self-loathing. In one of Rena's journal entries she describes her experience following a long day of classes, an hour of exercise, and nothing to eat all day. "While I was undressing to take a shower, I happened to glance in the mirror and had never looked so disgustingly fat. I freaked out and began to hyperventilate. All I could focus on was my walrus-sized gut. I didn't know what to do. There was nothing in my stomach to throw up so I cut my wrist. What I really wanted to do was to cut my stomach open and drain out whatever was in there making me fat. By cutting myself I was hoping that draining my blood would make me thinner."

Several of the women described going into trance prior to a binge. In her self portrait (Figure 2) Sophia explains that, "the spiral characterized the experience of a drowning kind of hypnotic thing, like falling into a tunnel, and where your mind goes away." Similarly, for Ana, "When I get very wound up there's something inside me that I feel like is not even me, that automatically sets in and I can't stop it. Its like I go into a trance and bingeing is all I can think about. Nothing's satisfied until the binge is over."

## Participants' Connection with One Another in the MBED Group

During the M-BED group, the women had the opportunity for the first time in their lives to connect and communicate with other women who had experienced symptoms of bulimia nervosa, depression, anxiety, and painful family relationships. For Ana, "The greatest part of the group was getting to know other people having similar problems so that I am not so alone or so bad. The fact that the other women in the M-BED group could listen to my story and not think I'm crazy or react negatively was helpful." The group became a safe container to hold all of their experiences as well a safe space in which to learn mindfulness meditation. According to Eva, "It broke the isolation and the secrecy. The time I spent with the other group members was the most valuable thing for me." Over the course of the group the women felt listened to, accepted, validated, and understood. This process, combined with the effects of meditation cultivated their ability to trust themselves and the other women in the group. As trust deepened, the women were able to reclaim and reveal more of their authentic selves with one another. Rena observed that, "I could look at the other women and see them as individuals and that helped me to see that I must be an individual too."

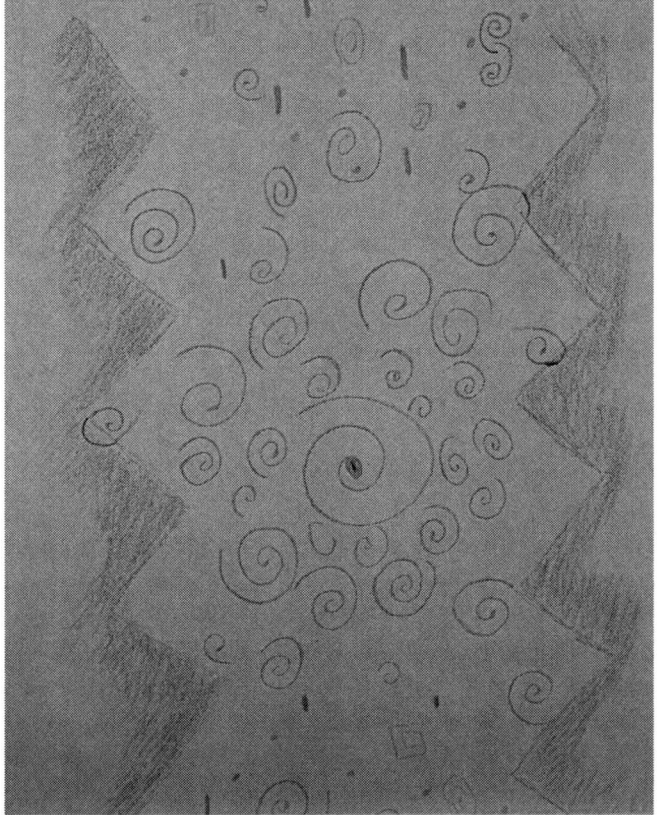

**FIGURE 2** Sophia's Post-Group Portrait: The Middle Way.

## Participants' Connection with Themselves Through Meditation

Within the context of the safety and acceptance of the M-BED group, mindfulness meditation, although challenging, provided a way for the women to become more self-aware and embodied. The women cultivated a practice that allowed them to observe themselves from a more cognitive perspective without their usual, extreme, emotional reactivity. The mini-meditation assisted them in lowering anxiety in their moment-to-moment experience allowing them to think about their experiences more clearly, thereby interrupting their automatic self-destructive patterns. Ruth finds herself repeating, "without judgment" throughout her day. "This has brought mindfulness to my day when I am feeling stressed. It helps ground me in the present, allows me to let go of judgment, and lowers my anxiety."

They creatively adapted the formal meditation practices to fit their lifestyle and personal needs. As a result of their meditation, the women described themselves as being more self-aware, self-accepting, assertive, hopeful, intimate with others, and differentiated from family. Conversely, they reported behaviors that were less impulsive, self-destructive, and out of control. Sophia describes, "My meditation practice has provided me with an opportunity to accept myself, although facing that space that is myself feels so scary. Although my sense of self is still pretty weak, I am willing to fight for my psychic space." Similarly, Rena has experienced, "The more I meditate, the more accepting I am towards myself and the easier it becomes not to judge my thoughts. When I can see the reality of myself, I don't have to try and hate myself and send myself away." For Kelley, "The meditation helped me to really slow down, stop and think, and reevaluate who I was and what I wanted out of life."

## Shifts in Sense of Self and Coping Strategies at the Conclusion of M-BED Group

### Eva

Since participating in the M-BED group, Eva reports, "I purged like a lot less, like a 700% reduction less. I haven't purged since I started group." Eva notes that she is more self aware of her actions and that she suspects this is directly responsible for lowering her impulsiveness to purge. Eva was able to practice and use the mini meditation. She found it helpful in lowering her anxiety and centering herself. She thought it allowed her to "take a moment to step back from a situation and get more insight before taking action." She commented that in regards to mindfulness, she was working toward becoming "calmer and a more inwardly compassionate person."

In her first self-portrait (Figure 3), Eva's face appeared quite fragmented and was composed of small bits of paper unevenly glued together. She presents only her face with the features misaligned and distorted. Eva explains, "There is no body beyond my head because my body is a source of self-consciousness best ignored." In her second self-portrait (Figure 4) her image is smoother and more integrated with her facial features in the right locations. Her neck and shoulders are visible.

### Kelly

By the end of the M-BED group, Kelley was beginning to accept that she was never going to be a thin, 16-year old girl again. In her second self-portrait (Figure 5) she has drawn a mirror image of herself with the two images holding hands to illustrate that she is moving toward a more realistic, integrated sense of self. "When I started this group I knew that I needed to make changes. The me I thought I was and the me my abusive partner said I was, were both distorted images reflecting back on each other like a prism or something, yeah, like a prison."

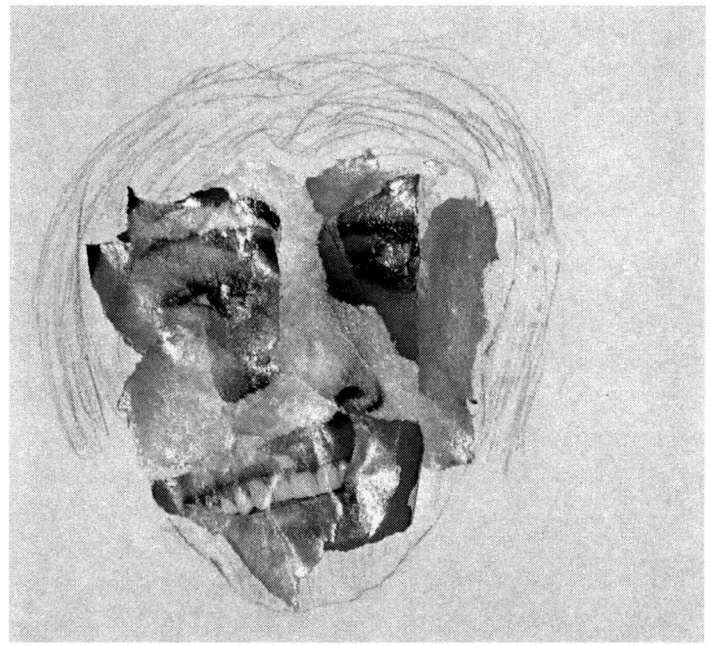

**FIGURE 3** Eva's Pre-Group Self Portrait.

**FIGURE 4** Eva's Post-Group Self Portrait.

RENA

"I wanted to be like a Barbie doll but I can't because, even at my thinnest, I have a certain bone size. I used to wake up in the morning and I'm just like "oh gosh, you look awful" because I'm expecting to see a size 4 in the

**FIGURE 5** Kelley's Post-Group Self Portrait.

mirror but I'm a size 10 or 12. I'm still figuring out who I am, but I'm not trying to squeeze myself into something mentally that I'm not" (Figure 6). "I've had it with being treated badly and treating myself badly. I am trying to love myself because that's where it's starting."

## SOPHIA

"As a feminist, I feel that my values and ideals are undermined by men and the culture and that leaves me feeling angry, which I don't want to feel. When I am aware of unpleasant situations, I don't like the feelings associated with them. When I am aware of pleasant events, I am already anticipating the loss of them and the associated unpleasant feelings of loss. I am able to notice all those things about myself and that is scary. I feel vulnerable to all outside life." (Figure 2) In addition, Sophia believes that one of the most significant changes she's made is separating from her "caustic mother situation." She has become increasingly aware of her mother's negative influence and that "my mother's perceptions of her body are not necessarily like right on the money. That is a huge deal for me."

**FIGURE 6** Rena's Post-Group Self Portrait.

RUTH

Ruth's central idea is one of optimism and "getting a fresh start in the sense of a new season." (Figure 7) She is moving toward thinking healthy and being good to herself. Ruth has unresolved issues in her family and decided to take a leave from school in order to address them. She is practicing ways

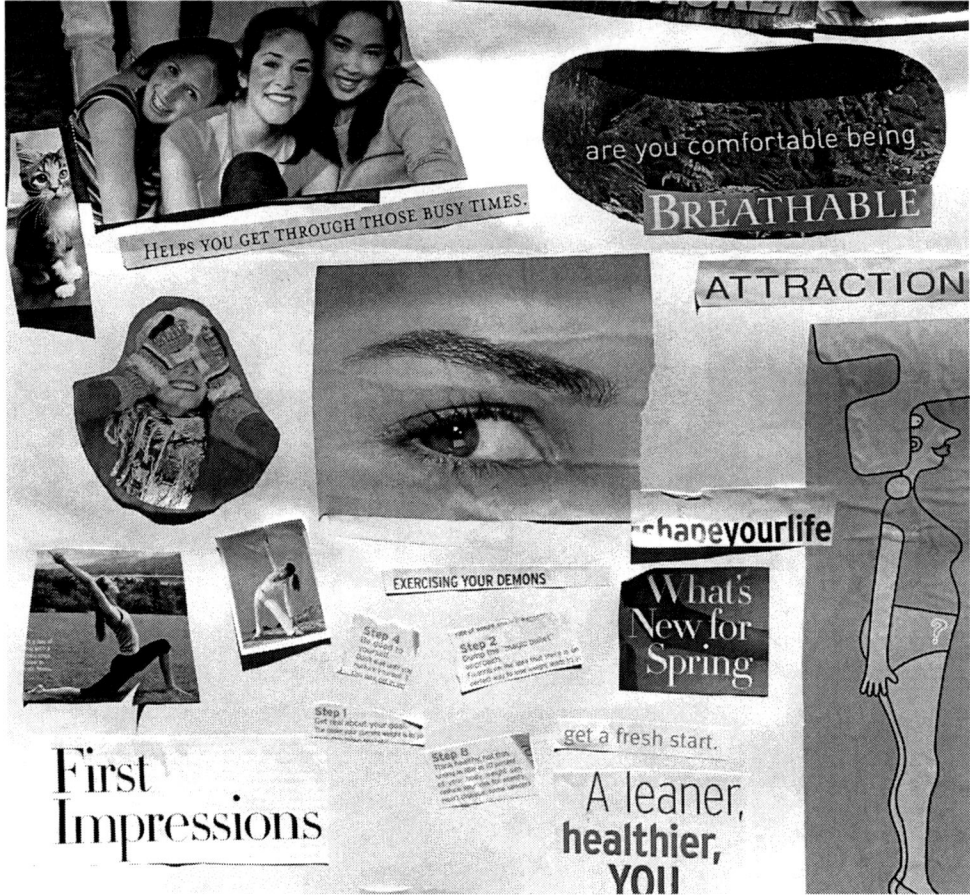

**FIGURE 7** Ruth's Post-Group Self-Portrait.

to take care of herself that are not self-destructive. She has a large eye in the center of her poster representing her continued wariness in trusting herself as well as others.

ANA

Ana lived with her abusive parents throughout the group. Her second self-portrait reflects that she is struggling with the notion of home. (Figure 8) She can more easily speak about the dog that "looks sad and lonely because he wants someone to pay attention to him." She intellectually recognizes that she alone must cultivate a feeling of home or love within herself. "I found that quote and while I know I have to do that, I just don't know how. I don't know how to separate from my parents. I don't know how to make a life or to be happy in myself. I feel like I am not my own person yet."

**FIGURE 8** Ana's Post-Group Self-Portrait.

For the six women participants, the core experience of the M-BED group involved a journey that began from a lonely, hate-filled relationship with a totally disconnected, disembodied, idealized, objectified image of self, to a relationship with the self that was curious, interested, aware, open, gentler, kinder, and more authentic. Developing a connection to their inner self allowed them to acknowledge and embrace their human vulnerability as well as that of the other women in the M-BED group. As the women were able to look deeply at and care for one another, they had a taste of the beauty and poignancy of human participation, the essence of relationship, the we-feeling in mutual vulnerability (Richards, Hardman & Berrett, 2007; Todres, 2004), diminishing their chronic sense of separation and isolation.

## CONCLUSIONS

The lived experiences of the participants in this study suggest that there is great potential for helping women recover from bulimia nervosa in the context of a structured, experiential, M-BED group. The combination of meditation practice, psychoeducation, and interpersonal approaches, provides a powerful intervention to build self-awareness, interpersonal connection, and positive coping skills, while reducing intense emotional reactivity, judgmental thoughts, and self-harming behaviors. Since the participants in this study were concurrently receiving individual psychotherapy, it is impossible to clearly separate out the specific effects of the M-BED group alone. As such, further research in this area to measure the degree of benefit, particularly for those women not responding to more traditional treatments, would be informative. For women with more severe eating disorder symptoms, it may be that an M-BED group would be a useful adjunct to individual or family psychotherapy. Alternatively, offering MBSR to younger women to enhance healthy self-awareness and coping might prevent the onset of self-harming behaviors such as bulimia nervosa.

While the M-BED group was a structured intervention, it is important that the facilitator have enough clinical experience to know when to let go of that structure, be in the moment, and allow process to unfold. Furthermore, it is essential that the facilitators of mindfulness-based interventions have their own meditation practice in order to model the mindful intentions and to help group members understand their experiences with meditation.

Mindfulness is not a cookbook technique. It is a transformational journey that, while secularized by Kabat-Zinn (1990), is nevertheless based on the psycho-spiritual beliefs of Buddhism. Although there are few studies exploring the impact of spirituality on recovery from an eating disorder (Crenshaw, 1998; Orbanic, 2001; Richards, Hardman, & Berrett, 2007; Smith, Hardman, Richards, & Fischer, 2003), this is an important question for further research and the development of effective treatment interventions for individuals with eating disorders.

## REFERENCES

American Psychiatric Association. (2000). *Diagnostic and statistical manual of mental disorders, fourth edition, text revision.* Washington, DC: Author.

Bennett-Goleman, T. (2001). *Emotional alchemy: How the mind can heal the heart.* New York: Harmony Books.

Bishop, S. R. (2002). What do we really know about mindfulness-based stress reduction? *Psychosomatic Medicine, 64,* 71–84.

Brown, L. M., & Gilligan, C. (1992). *Meeting at the crossroads.* New York: Ballantine Books.

Bruch, H. (1988). *Conversations with anorexics.* New York: Basic Books.

Crenshaw, C. R. (1998). The experience of women who participated in an eating disorder treatment program designed to develop a feminist consciousness. (Doctoral Dissertation, Georgia State University, 1998). *Dissertation Abstracts International, B59/11,* 5783, May 1999.

Dalai Lama & Goleman, D. (2003). *Destructive emotions: How can we overcome them?* New York: Bantam Books.

Depraz, N., Varela, F. J., & Vermersch, P. (2003). *On becoming aware: A pragmatics of experiencing.* Philadelphia: John Benjamins Publishing Company.

Drew, N. (1999). A return to Husserl and researcher self-awareness. In E. C. Polifroni & M. Welch (Eds.), *Perspectives on philosophy of science in nursing: An historical and contemporary anthology* (pp. 263–272). Philadelphia: Lippincott, Williams, & Wilkins.

Drew, N. (2001). Meaningfulness as an epistemologic concept for explicating the researcher's constitutive part in phenomenologic research. *Advances in Nursing Science, 23*(4), 16–31.

Drew, N. (2004). Developing a synthesis of intentionality: The role of the bracketing facilitator. *Advances in Nursing Science, 27*(3), 215–223.

Fairburn, C. G., Agras, W. S., & Wilson, G. T. (1992). The research on the treatment of bulimia nervosa: Practical and theoretical implications. In G. H. Anderson & S.H. Kennedy (Eds.), *The biology of feast and famine: Relevance to eating disorders* (pp. 317–340). San Diego: Academic Press.

Fairburn, C. G., & Cooper, P. J. (1982). Self-induced vomiting and bulimia nervosa: An undetected problem. *British Medical Journal, 284*, 1153–1155.

Fisher, M., Golden, N. H., Katzman, D. K. et al. (1995). Eating disorders in adolescents: A background paper. *Journal of Adolescent Health, 16*, 420–437.

Fleming, V., Gaidys, U., & Robb, Y. (2003). Hermeneutic research in nursing: eveloping a Gadamerian-based research method. *Nursing Inquiry, 10*(2), 113–120.

Garfinkel, P. E., Moldofsky, H., & Garner, D. M. (1980). The heterogeneity of anorexia nervosa. *Archives of General Psychiatry, 37*, 1036–1040.

Hanh, T. N. (1975). *The miracle of mindfulness*. Boston: Beacon Press.

Hsu, L. K. G., Crisp, A. H., & Harding, B. (1979). Outcome of anorexia nervosa. *Lancet, i*, 61–65.

Husserl, E. (1983). *Ideas pertaining to a pure phenomenology and to a henomenological philosophy, first book* (F. Kersten, Trans.). Boston: Kluwer Academic Publishers. (Original work published 1913).

Jhally, S. (Producer/Director/Editor) & Kilbourne, J. (Writer). (1995). *Slim Hopes* [video documentary]. Northampton, Massachusetts: Media Education Foundation.

Kabat-Zinn, J. (1990). *Full catastrophe living*. New York: Bantam Doubleday Dell Publishing Group, Inc.

Kabat-Zinn, J. (1994). *Wherever you go, there you are*. New York: Hyperion.

Kabat-Zinn, J., Massion, A. O., Kristeller, J., Peterson, L. G., Fletcher, K. E., Pbert, L., Lenderking, W. R., & Santorelli, S. F. (1992). Effectiveness of a meditation-based stress reduction program in the treatment of anxiety disorders. *American Journal of Psychiatry, 149*(7), 936–943.

Kristeller, J. L., & Hallett, C. B. (1999). An exploratory study of a meditation-based intervention for binge eating disorder. *Journal of Health Psychology, 4*(3), 357–363.

Mason, O., & Hargreaves, I. (2001). A qualitative study of mindfulness-based cognitive therapy for depression. *British Journal of Medical Psychology, 74*, 197–212.

Miller, J. J., Fletcher, K., & Kabat-Zinn, J. (1995). Three year follow-up and clinical implications of a mindfulness mediation-based stress reduction intervention in the treatment of anxiety disorder. *General Hospital Psychiatry, 17*, 192–200.

Naidus, B. (1993). *One size does not fit all*. Littleton, Colorado: Aigis Publications.

National Eating Disorders Association. (2006). General Eating Disorders Information: Facts for Activists. Retrieved March 23, 2006, from http://www.edap.org/p.asp?WebPage_ID=320&Profile_ID=95634.

Orbanic, S. D. (2001). A phenomenological study of self-love in women's experiences healing from bulimia. (Doctoral dissertation, University of Connecticut, 2001). *Dissertation Abstracts International, B62/02*, 783, August, 2001.

Pipher, M. (1994). *Reviving Ophelia: Saving the selves of adolescent girls*. New York: Ballantine Books.

Proulx, K. (2003). Integrating mindfulness-based stress reduction. *Holistic Nursing Practice, 17*(4), 201–208.

Richards, P. S., Hardman, R. K., & Berrett, M. E. (2007). *Spiritual approaches in the treatment of women with eating disorders*. Washington, DC: American Psychological Association.

Roth, B., & Creaser, T. (1997). Mindfulness meditation-based stress reduction: Experience with a bilingual inner-city population. *The Nurse Practitioner 22*(3), 150–176.

Santorelli, S. (1992). *A qualitative case analysis of mindfulness meditation training in an outpatient stress reduction clinic and its implications for the development of self- knowledge*. Unpublished doctoral dissertation, University of Massachusetts at Amherst.

Segal, Z. V., Williams, J. M. G., & Teasdale, J. D. (2002). *Mindfulness-based cognitive therapy for depression: A new approach to preventing relapse*. New York: The Guilford Press.

Shapiro, S. L., Schwartz, G. E., & Bonner, G. (1998). Effects of mindfulness-based stress reduction on medical and premedical students. *Journal of Behavioral Medicine, 21*(6), 581–599.

Smith, F. T., Hardman, R. K., Richards, P. S., & Fischer, L. (2003). Intrinsic eligiousness and spiritual well-being as predictors of treatment outcome among women with eating disorders. *Eating Disorders: The Journal of Treatment and Prevention, 11*, 15–26.

Stice, E. (1999). Clinical implications of psychosocial research on bulimia nervosa and binge-eating disorder. *Journal Clinical Psychology, 55*, 675–683.

Todres, L. (2004). The wound that connects: A consideration of "narcissism" and the creation of a soulful space. *The Indo-Pacific Journal of Phenomenology, 4*(1), 1–12.

van Manen, M. (1990). *Researching lived experience: Human science for an action sensitive pedagogy*. Ontario, Canada: Althouse Press.

# Adding Mindfulness to CBT Programs for Binge Eating: A Mixed-Methods Evaluation

HANNAH WOOLHOUSE

*Healthy Mothers Healthy Families Research Group, Murdoch Children's Research Institute, Royal Children's Hospital, Parkville, Victoria, Australia*

ANN KNOWLES

*Faculty of Life and Social Sciences, Swinburne University of Technology, Hawthorn, Victoria, Australia*

NAOMI CRAFTI

*FedUp?, Melbourne, Victoria, Australia*

*The current study investigated the effectiveness of a combined mindfulness-CBT group therapy program for women with binge eating problems. Questionnaires were completed by group participants pre-program (n = 30), post-program (n = 30) and 3 month follow-up (n = 28). Significant reductions between pre- and post-program scores were found on standardised measures assessing binge eating, dieting, and body image dissatisfaction, with all reductions maintained at follow-up. Qualitative interviews with 16 women following completion of the program revealed*

We are very grateful to all of the women who took part in the Mindful MEG program and contributed their time to the research project. Women who took part in the qualitative interviews contributed significant time to share their thoughts and experiences with us. Many thanks also to the Mindful MEG group facilitators, who were tireless in their efforts to provide a valuable group experience to participants, and who also contributed their time and energy to the research project. We are also grateful to colleagues who have read and given feedback on the research at various stages of the drafting process: Diane Mainwarring, Greg Murray, and Stephanie J. Brown.

The study was approved by the Swinburne University Human Research Ethics Committee (SUHREC Project 0607/021). Written informed consent was obtained from all participants. This publication was supported by the Victorian Government's Operational Infrastructure Support Program.

*the value of mindfulness in improving eating behaviour through increased self-awareness. This exploratory study supports the value of adding mindfulness to the more commonly utilised CBT-based programs for binge eating.*

Eating disorders remain a serious concern in modern Australian society (Hay, Mond, Buttner, & Darby, 2008). Both bulimia nervosa (BN) and binge eating disorder (BED) involve significant problems with binge eating episodes (American Psychiatric Association, 2000). Sub-clinical eating problems may also involve episodes of binge eating which cause significant distress (American Psychiatric Association, 2000). Women who have problems with binge eating are significantly more likely to suffer from low self-esteem (Sanftner & Crowther, 1998), poor body image (Isnard et al., 2003), interpersonal problems (Eldredge, Locke, & Horowitz, 1998), depression, and anxiety (Isnard et al., 2003).

Cognitive behavioural therapy (CBT) for binge eating (Fairburn, Marcus, & Wilson, 1993) remains the "gold standard" treatment for both BN and BED in reducing binge eating frequency and severity, compensatory behaviours, dietary restraint, and body image dissatisfaction (Brownley, Berkman, Sedway, Lohr, & Bulik, 2007; Shapiro et al., 2007). However, many participants do not achieve full abstinence from binge eating following CBT, with studies consistently showing that around 50% of participants remain symptomatic at the end of treatment and at 5 years follow-up (Wilson, 1996). Average drop-out rates of around 25% (Shapiro et al., 2007) are also relatively high, suggesting that a significant proportion of individuals do not find benefit in the cognitive-behavioural approach. Multi-faceted or eclectic treatment approaches are one way of potentially helping more clients.

Mindfulness is a relatively new approach to the treatment of binge eating difficulties, and may prove a beneficial addition to the traditional CBT-based approaches. Based in Buddhist philosophy, mindfulness involves bringing one's attention to the present moment in a particular way—on purpose, and with non-judgemental acceptance (Kabat-Zinn, 1990). Mindfulness is considered relevant to many of the factors implicated in the development and maintenance of eating disorders, such as emotion regulation (Dalai Lama & Goleman, 2003), depression (Segal, Williams & Teasdale, 2002), anxiety (Miller, Fletcher, & Kabat-Zinn, 1995), self-esteem (Roth & Creaser, 1997), and quality of life (Carlson, Speca, Patel, & Goodey, 2003).

One of the first studies to explore the use of mindfulness in the treatment of binge eating (Kristeller & Hallett, 1999) examined the efficacy of a 6-week meditation-based group treatment program for 21 obese women who met the criteria for BED, finding a significant decrease in bingeing frequency. The authors concluded that mindfulness meditation may be an effective addition to the treatment for BED, through its ability to improve emotion regulation and enhance self-awareness. Subsequent studies have found similar results, with significant reductions to binge eating, food pre-occupation, body image concerns, and increased control of eating behaviour (Baer, Fischer, & Huss, 2005; Hepworth, 2010).

While these preliminary studies have provided tentative support for the effectiveness of mindfulness-based programs in reducing binge eating frequency, severity, and body image dissatisfaction, more evidence of effectiveness is needed. Further qualitative research is also needed to explore the lived experience of mindfulness-based therapies for binge eating, and the mechanisms of change through which mindfulness may help women with binge eating problems.

The current study used a mixed methods approach to provide a comprehensive picture of the changes experienced by women following participation in a combined mindfulness-CBT group therapy program for women with binge eating.


## METHOD

### Participants

Fifty-four women completed an assessment interview between June 2006 and June 2008 and 43 chose to take part in the program (through 6 separate groups). Of the 43 women who started the Mindful Moderate Eating Group (MEG) program, 38 agreed to take part in the research project. Five women withdrew at some stage during the program, leaving 33 eligible participants. Thirty completed a pre- and post-questionnaire, and 28 completed a follow-up questionnaire 3 months after completion of the program. At the time of enrolment, 31% of participants exhibited symptoms of BN, 50% percent showed symptoms of BED, and the remaining 19% percent reported symptoms of a sub-clinical level. Sixteen women completed a qualitative interview following completion of the program.


### Study Design

The current study was a repeated-measures evaluation of the effectiveness of the Mindful Moderate Eating Group (MEG) program. An effectiveness study aims to evaluate a program in a naturalistic setting, which may reflect the realities of psychotherapy as it is practiced in the real world. This "real world" of psychotherapy is often flexible, messy, and unpredictable and significantly different from the strict parameters set by randomised controlled trials (Seligman, 1995). The current study aimed to change as little as possible about the way the Mindful MEG program was being provided through the University Psychology Clinic. There was no randomisation of clients to treatment and control groups, and women who fit diagnoses of BN, BED, and EDNOS were included, as were women with co-morbid *DSM-IV-R* disorders (American Psychiatric Association, 2000). Facilitators were encouraged to adapt the treatment manual to fit their personal style, and the specific needs of their particular group. Each Mindful MEG program was facilitated by two female postgraduate psychology students (a lead facilitator and a co-facilitator). The lead facilitator of the program was expected to have significant experience in the practice of mindfulness (i.e., to have their own current personal practice, and to have undergone a period of meditation as extensive as that expected of group participants).

## Mindful Moderate Eating Group

The MEG program (Crafti, 1994) was rewritten in 2005 to incorporate a significant mindfulness component (Crafti & Peyton, 2005). The resulting Mindful MEG program is a group therapy program for women with binge eating difficulties incorporating both mindfulness and CBT components. CBT techniques (such as regular eating, planned meals, and food monitoring) are introduced to explore triggers for binge episodes, and restore regularity to eating patterns. Mindfulness practices (such as mindful eating, formal sitting meditation, and informal mindfulness practices) are introduced to encourage awareness of the factors surrounding binge eating such as emotional distress, perfectionism, negative thought patterns, hunger and satiety cues, and body image disturbance. Program sessions ran for 3 hours for 10 consecutive weeks, with a follow-up session 3 months after the tenth session. Each session followed a fairly uniform structure: check in; main mindfulness practice and discussion; discussion of home practices; weekly topic, brief mindfulness practice. Table 1 provides a more detailed outline of the weekly structure of the Mindful MEG program.

## Procedure

Recruitment occurred via an advertisement on the University Psychology Clinic website. Referrals to the program were also received from individual counsellors working at the Psychology Clinic, as well as the Eating Disorders Foundation of Victoria, General Practitioners in the community, and previous MEG participants. A group size of eight was considered ideal (Yalom, 1995), but group size ranged from six to nine participants. All potential group participants were invited to take part in the research project at the time of the assessment interview. Willing participants were asked to complete a Research Project consent form outlining the entailments of participation. Ethics approval for the research evaluation project was provided by the University Human Research Ethics Committee.

Minimal exclusion criteria were employed in the current study: anorexia nervosa, extreme drug or alcohol use, severe suicidal ideation, male gender, age under 18 years, or significant personality issues which would preclude productive group work. Where exclusion criteria were present, women were offered individual counselling.

**TABLE 1** Weekly Structure of the Mindful MEG Program

| Session number | Session description |
| --- | --- |
| Session 1 | • Group introduction<br>• Introduction to mindfulness (raising exercise)<br>• Body scan and discussion<br>• Introduction to CBT model of binge eating (food monitoring) |
| Session 2 | • Body scan and discussion<br>• Regular eating and meal planning |
| Session 3 | • Sitting meditation and discussion<br>• Thought defusion exercises<br>• Perfectionism |
| Session 4 | • Sitting meditation and discussion<br>• Coping with emotions (including grounding and self soothing) |
| Session 5 | • Sitting meditation and discussion<br>• Identifying and labelling emotions<br>• Introducing forbidden foods to your meal plans |
| Session 6 | • Loving-kindness meditation and discussion<br>• Self-esteem |
| Session 7 | • Walking meditation and discussion<br>• Assertiveness and anger |
| Session 8 | • Lake meditation and discussion<br>• The socio-cultural context of eating and body image |
| Session 9 | • Sitting meditation and discussion<br>• Relapse prevention plans |
| Session 10 | • Sitting meditation and discussion<br>• Finishing up activities |

## Quantitative Data Collection

Quantitative data was collected via a 17-page questionnaire booklet completed by participants at three separate time points—prior to the first session (pre-program questionnaire), following completion of the tenth session (post-program questionnaire), and at the 3 month follow-up meeting (3 month follow-up questionnaire).

OUTCOME MEASURES INCLUDED IN QUANTITATIVE
QUESTIONNAIRES

Demographic features of participants were obtained in the pre-program questionnaire and included age, highest level of education achieved, employment status, current occupation, marital status, number of children, and country of birth.

The frequency of binge eating and compensatory behaviours was measured using a table from the Eating Disorders Inventory-3 Symptom Checklist (EDI-3-SC; Garner, 2004), a self-report table which asks about the frequency of binge eating, over the last 3 months. In validation studies, the EDI-3 has shown satisfactory internal consistency and excellent sensitivity and specificity (Clausen, Rosenvinge, Friborg, & Rokkedal, 2011).

The Multifactorial Assessment of Eating Disorders Scale (MAEDS) contains 56 items and was designed to evaluate treatment outcome for anorexia and bulimia (Anderson, Williamson, Duchmann, Gleaves, & Barbin, 1999). It includes six subscales—Binge Eating, Purgative Behaviour, Fear of Fatness, Restrictive Eating, Avoidance of Forbidden Foods, and Depression. Test retest reliability (Anderson et al., 1999) and criterion validity of the MAEDS have been supported (Martin, Williamson, & Thaw, 2000).

The Dutch Eating Behaviour Questionnaire (DEBQ; van Strien, Frijters, Bergers, & Defares, 1986) is commonly used in research on binge eating, and contains three subscales related to three different types of overeating (Restrained Eating, Emotional Eating, and External Eating). The DEBQ has shown excellent factorial validity, high internal consistency, satisfactory-good reliability, and satisfactory concurrent and discriminant validity (van Strien, Engels, Van Leeuwe, & Snoek, 2005).

The Ben-Tovim Walker Body Attitudes Questionnaire (BAQ; Ben-Tovim & Walker, 1991) was developed specifically to measure the broad range of attitudes women hold towards their bodies. The BAQ has shown good convergent validity as well as satisfactory reliability (Ben-Tovim & Walker, 1991). Due to low Chronbach's alpha levels found in the current study, only two subscales were included in further analyse: Feelings of Fatness and Body-disparagement.

The Eating Self-Efficacy Scale (ESES; Glynn & Ruderman, 1986) contains 25 items and is conceptually based on Bandura's (1977) model of self-efficacy. The ESES measures an individual's perceived ability to control their eating behaviour in a range of situations (i.e., after work, when preparing food, when depressed). The scale shows high internal consistency coefficients for a sample of female undergraduates, and acceptable test-retest reliability (Glynn & Ruderman, 1986).

The Emotional Overeating Questionnaire (EOQ; Masheb & Grilo, 2006) measures the frequency of overeating in response to six specific emotions: anxiety; sadness; loneliness; tiredness; anger; happiness. A total EOQ score is used rather than six separate scores, with a higher score reflecting more emotional overeating. The EOQ shows adequate test-retest reliability and internal consistency (Masheb & Grilo, 2006).

The Cognitive and Affective Mindfulness Scale-Revised (CAMS-R; Feldman, Hayes, Kumar, Greeson, & Laurenceau, 2007) contains 12 items and assesses four separate dimensions of mindfulness: Awareness; Attention; Present-Focus; and Acceptance. Acceptable levels of internal consistency have been found for the overall CAMS-R score, but not the separate subscales, and because of this only the total score is used in the current analyses (Baer, Smith, Hopkins, Krietemeyer, & Toney, 2006).

Quantitative questionnaires administered following group participation (the post-program questionnaire and the follow-up questionnaire) included the above measures plus additional questions on amount of time spent in formal meditation practice in the last 3 months. The post-program questionnaire also included a single-item, open-ended question asking what aspects of the program participants found most helpful.

## Qualitative Data Collection

At the conclusion of the tenth session of the program, all participants were invited to take part in an in-depth interview to explore their experiences in the program. While semi-structured in nature, the interviewer was encouraged to follow participants to the topics most salient for them. General topics to guide the interview included: aspects of the program that were helpful, or challenging; experiences of specific mindfulness and CBT practices; what changed for participants during the program as a result of participating in the program; and what changes they attributed to mindfulness practice. All qualitative interviews were recorded and transcribed, and a separate consent form was completed for this component of the study.

## Data Analysis

Multivariate Analysis of Variance (MANOVA) was considered the most appropriate statistical test due to the large number of outcome variables and risk of a Type I error. Outcome variables were arranged into four groups based on conceptual links, resulting in four one-way repeated measures MANOVAs with an alpha level of .05. For significant MANOVAs, univariate ANOVA results for each individual outcome variable are reported. In the case of a significant univariate ANOVA test, post hoc tests to determine the exact location of the significant differences were completed, using repeated contrasts. Effect sizes are reported via partial eta squared. Qualitative data analysis was conducted via the Interpretative Phenomenologcial Analysis method (Smith & Osborne, 2008). Ten percent of the interview transcripts were cross-coded by an independent psychologist to ensure agreement of relevant themes.

# RESULTS

## Demographic Details

Of the 43 women who began the Mindful MEG program, 5 withdrew at some point, giving a drop-out rate of 12%. The sample was a highly educated one, with 80% having completed a university degree. Around 50% of participants were in full-time employment, and 26% were in part-time employment. Seventeen percent of participants were currently studying.

Fifty-seven percent of the sample was currently single, while 31% of participants had children. The age of the sample ranged from 18 to 52 years ($M = 32.2$ years, $SD = 7.9$).

## Engagement With Mindfulness Practices

The amount of formal mindfulness practice reported by participants at the completion of the program and at the 3-month follow-up is presented in Figure 1.

Reported engagement in formal mindfulness practice was high during the 10 week program, with 90% practicing some level of formal mindfulness practice while taking part in the program. While the levels of meditation dropped following the program, over half of the participants were still engaging in formal meditation practice at the 3-month follow-up.

## Quantitative Findings

A binge frequency of twice a week or more, for at least 3 months, is required for a *DSM-IV-TR* diagnosis of BN or BED. Figure 2 shows the percentage of participants who reported binge eating twice a week or more over the last 3 months, as measured by the EDI-3-SC. The percentage of participants reporting binge eating at least twice a week or more dropped from 80% prior to the program, down to 14% at the 3 month follow-up.

Table 2 reports the main quantitative findings. Four MANOVAs found a significant improvement in scores between pre- and post-program for (a) general eating psychopathology, (b) overeating behaviour, (c) dieting behaviour, and (d) body image dissatisfaction. The results of post-hoc

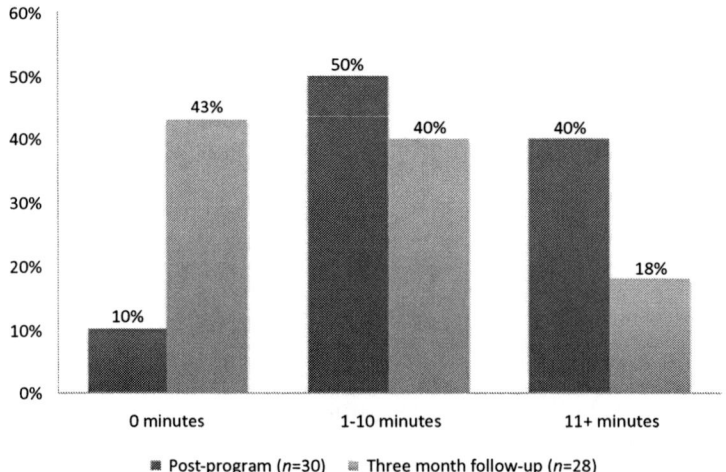

**FIGURE 1** Average time spent in formal meditation practice per day.

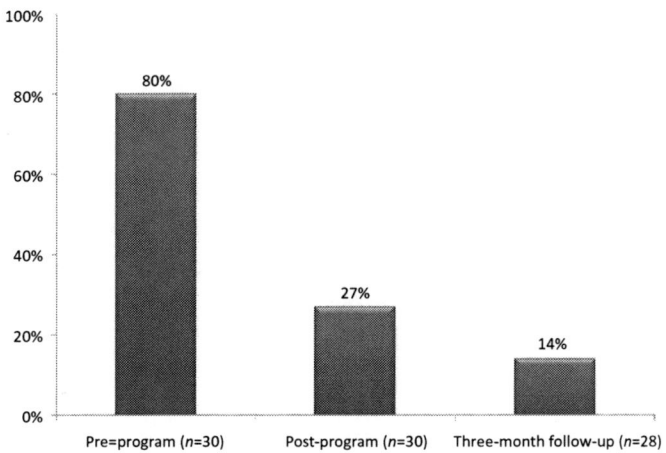

**FIGURE 2** Binge eating twice a week or more in the last three months.

ANOVAs are also provided in Table 2, and show significant improvements on each of the individual scales. All improvements were maintained at 3-month follow-up.

Scores on the CAMS-R mindfulness scale increased over the course of the research project: $M = 26.97$ at pre-program, $M = 29.30$ at post-program, and $M = 30.04$ at the 3 month follow-up. A repeated measures ANOVA revealed a significant difference between pre and post-program scores: $F(1.63) = 4.89$; $p = .010$, partial eta squared $= 0.16$.

In the post-program questionnaire, participants were asked to comment on what aspect of the program was most helpful to them (see Table 3). Reducing these categories to more broad groupings reveals that group environment factors were the most frequently reported as "most helpful," accounting for 50% of items. Mindfulness related factors were the next most commonly listed, accounting for 30% of responses, followed by CBT factors which accounted for 19% of responses.

## Qualitative Findings

It is beyond the scope of this article to present all the findings from the qualitative interviews; the focus will be on the value of mindfulness as identified by group participants.

### CHANGES ATTRIBUTED TO MINDFULNESS

*Reduced bingeing through mindful eating.* Of all the mindfulness practices introduced during the program, mindful eating was identified by interviewees as the most helpful. Participants were asked to eat at least one

**TABLE 2** Changes to Outcome Measures

| | Pre-program | Post-program | Follow-up | | | | Partial eta |
|---|---|---|---|---|---|---|---|
| | $N = 30$ | $N = 30$ | $N = 28$ | | | | square |
| | M (SD) | M (SD) | M (SD) | F | p | df | |
| **Eating psychopathology** | | | | | | | |
| Manova 1 | | | | 6.70 | .00 | 6, 20 | .67 |
| MAEDS total[a, b] | 2.69 (0.72) | 1.97 (0.73) | 2.01 (0.78) | 19.91 | .00 | 2 | .44 |
| DEBQ total[a, b] | 3.00 (0.57) | 2.45 (0.71) | 2.25 (0.61) | 19.84 | .00 | 2 | .44 |
| ESES total[a, b] | 4.97 (0.97) | 4.28 (1.29) | 4.01 (1.33) | 6.57 | .00 | 2 | .29 |
| **Overeating** | | | | | | | |
| Manova 2 | | | | 7.63 | .00 | 8, 17 | .78 |
| MAEDS Binge eating[a, b] | 4.49 (0.87) | 2.85 (1.21) | 2.86 (1.28) | 39.37 | .00 | 2 | .62 |
| DEBQ Emotional eating[a, b] | 3.55 (0.79) | 2.85 (1.11) | 2.58 (1.05) | 17.60 | .00 | 2 | .42 |
| DEBQ External eating[a, b] | 3.02 (0.81) | 2.56 (0.91) | 2.36 (0.72) | 14.98 | .00 | 2 | .38 |
| EOQ[a, b] | 1.74 (0.99) | 1.07 (0.87) | 0.96 (1.10) | 16.78 | .00 | 2 | .41 |
| **Dieting** | | | | | | | |
| Manova 3 | | | | 3.17 | .02 | 6, 22 | .46 |
| MAEDS Restrictive eating[a, b] | 1.56 (1.13) | 1.04 (0.95) | 1.13 (0.88) | 7.32 | .01 | 2 | .21 |
| MAEDS Forbidden foods[a, b] | 2.38 (1.14) | 1.88 (0.95) | 1.13 (0.88) | 10.26 | .00 | 2 | .28 |
| DEBQ Restrained eating[a, b] | 2.25 (0.99) | 1.80 (0.86) | 1.72 (0.75) | 9.50 | .00 | 2 | .26 |
| **Body image dissatisfaction** | | | | | | | |
| Manova 4 | | | | 3.85 | .01 | 6, 21 | .52 |
| BAQ Feeling fat[a, b] | 4.21 (0.58) | 3.79 (0.57) | 3.79 (0.67) | 9.61 | .00 | 2 | .27 |
| BAQ body disparagement[a, b] | 3.05 (0.69) | 2.56 (0.62) | 2.67 (0.76) | 10.04 | .00 | 2 | .28 |
| MAEDS fear of weight gain[a, b] | 3.82 (1.04) | 3.07 (1.03) | 3.11 (1.13) | 9.41 | .00 | 2 | .27 |

*Note.* MAEDS = Multifactorial Assessment of Eating Disorders Scale, DEBQ = Dutch Eating Behaviour Questionnaire, ESES = Eating Self Efficacy Scale, EOQ = Emotional Overeating Questionnaire.

a = Significant difference between pre-program and post-program means.

b = No significant difference between post-program and follow-up means.

**TABLE 3** Most Helpful Aspects of the Mindful MEG Program ($n = 30$)

| Program component | Frequency |
|---|---|
| Support/learning from the group | 20* |
| Mindfulness generally/meditation | 19″ |
| Practical aspects of the program (i.e., time of sessions) | 9* |
| The facilitators | 7* |
| Regular eating | 6+ |
| Food monitoring | 5+ |
| Mindful eating | 5″ |
| 3-minute breathing space | 5″ |
| Strategies for coping with emotions | 5+ |
| Reading materials provided | 5* |
| Learning about oneself | 4* |
| The combination of mindfulness and CBT | 3* |
| Meal planning | 2+ |
| Total | 95 |

NB. Participants could provide more than one response for this question.
*Group environment factors.
″Mindfulness factors.
+CBT factors.

meal a day mindfully; slowing down the speed of their eating and paying attention to the sensory experience of eating. Slowing down the speed of eating provided more control, more awareness of feelings of hunger and fullness, and insights about likes and dislikes particularly in relation to "binge foods." This practice in particular was linked directly to changes in binge eating frequency and severity.

> For a very long time I recognised that I ate too quickly. And through diets and all sorts of things I had tried to consciously slow down. And it didn't happen for me until I thought about eating mindfully. . . . And I've found that I've really slowed down without sort of noticing it, and actually eat the food rather than inhaling it. (Abbey)

> I think that practicing the mindful eating, that was a huge one for me too, because um, some things I didn't even know what they tasted like. . . . I thought I loved liquorice, and I could devour it without really noticing what I was doing . . . and it was like, when I ate it "Oh, this has got a burning taste, it's disgusting." I actually didn't enjoy it. I actually threw the rest of it away after the exercise. And I'm finding that if I do the mindful eating, I eat a lot slower, I get full a lot quicker, I'm more satisfied. (Victoria)

*Improved quality of life.* Unrelated to food and eating, several participants identified positive changes to their interpersonal relationships and to their general sense of well-being, related specifically to the practice of mindfulness.

It's made a big difference . . . I was getting very depressed about just life in general, and I think that if you take away the past, to some extent, and you take away the future, then, basically you've got to enjoy right now. And so it's a lot lighter journey, because there's so much less baggage . . . I'm finding it actually a really beneficial way to just get through life. (Sasha)

I think it just really improves my general well-being, and my emotional state is a lot happier than before. With the meditations that I do, I just don't seem to get the down feeling which I used to have before. (Carrie)

And so many people have even commented on it. Like people who know that I'm doing this, but not that it's associated with an eating disorder. And certainly my family, and my sister in particular, who's pretty much my best friend, she says it all the time "You're different. You've really taken this mindfulness on board, like I can see it in you. And can you please teach it to me?" (Deena)

Many women also spoke of an increased ability to regulate their emotions, and to calm themselves down during times of distress.

It has relaxed me a lot more, and stopped me worrying about the future, and sort of feeling like I can still go after what I want, but whatever will be will be as well. (Wendy)

I think it's made a huge difference. I feel like I'm much more balanced, I feel like the minute something gets a bit stressful I can use some of the mindful techniques and defuse the situation. (Yvette)

MECHANISMS OF CHANGE

*Being in the present moment.* Spending more time in the present moment was identified by many women as having a significant and positive impact on their wellbeing.

We spend 90% of our time worrying about what's been, or what's not going to happen. And it's doing the meditation that made me realise my head is just in overdrive about, just crap, absolute crap . . . So now I'm finding that when my head goes to those places I'm like "Stop! What's happening now?" And try to focus on the, you know, if I'm doing the dishes, then just focus on that. (Victoria)

Basically, that Jon Kabat-Zinn saying you've got to live in every moment, because two weeks time may not come. You could be dead. You never know what could change so just live. It's making me practice more living in the moment, and not worrying about what is out of my control. (Geena)

## Movement From Avoidance to Awareness

All of the participants interviewed spoke of the value of increased awareness, and more specifically, the movement from avoidance to awareness.
For many women, the avoidance of thoughts, emotions, or physical sensations had led them to their current problems. Being asked to purposely
focus on their experience, including these feared internal experiences, was
confronting but beneficial. A movement towards awareness was the main
mechanism of change through which mindfulness operated.

> Beforehand I didn't take notice of what my emotions were, I just went
> by in a daze without really connecting or thinking about my feelings and
> emotions and during the 10 weeks I really honed in on those things.
> (Carrie)

> Just total awareness, across the board. Of everything. Just *awareness*.
> Of all the different things. To be aware of what you're feeling, what
> you're doing, what's happening around you. Just awareness of how
> you're not nurturing yourself, just awareness of everything that you're
> doing in your life that's not necessarily good for you. (Victoria)

> I think that mindfulness really helped to increase just awareness in gen-
> eral. Sort of taking that time out to go "How am I actually feeling?" I
> think that was really useful in putting me back into touch with, not just
> how I'm feeling physically, but emotionally as well. (Erica)

## Gaining Control and Choice

Following on from these new levels of awareness, participants found that
they were able to gain more control over their lives and behaviours.
Rather than being stuck on auto-pilot, participants were able to make more
considered and thoughtful choices.

> And now that I'm aware of it, then I'm able to do something different,
> 'cause I know that's what I'm doing now. So that was really good. (Erica)

> But it did give me enlightenment as to how to come round, you know,
> like it helped me back track a bit more about triggers and things. It sort
> of gives you more choice about things, like next time, you have more
> choices as to how to react or make a rational—I hate the word rational—
> but you kind of make a more thoughtful choice. (Rita)

## Movement From Self-Punishment to Self-Kindness

A common theme in the interviews was a change in the way women perceived and treated themselves. Previously, women had been harsh, critical,

and perfectionistic in their judgements of self. Participation in the group seemed to lead to a softening of these harsh judgements, and an increased understanding of the need to take care of oneself.

> Before I was so negative about every aspect of myself, from the physical to my personality. And during the 10 weeks I did start to notice that I wasn't so vicious with myself anymore, which was really good. (Carrie)

> I think a lot of us were perfectionists, when we began. Some are still, and some are less, and I'd say I'm much less now. It doesn't have to be all right, and I'm ok with that now, and that's something that I've really learnt. I don't need to judge myself, I don't care how I look, I don't care as much about how I appear to others, if I'm successful, whatever. And I don't want to continuously try to please others. I need to please myself, and if in turn others are happy with that, fine, and if not, too bad. (Yvette)

> That kind of like patience that you have during that time [when practicing mindfulness], transfers to patience with yourself and being more forgiving of yourself. I can't think of specific examples but I think generally there is an attitude of being a bit more gentle towards myself, and I think that was partly to do with the mindfulness. (Rita)

## DISCUSSION

The results of this exploratory study support the effectiveness of a combined mindfulness-CBT group therapy program for women with binge eating problems. Following participation in the program, significant reductions were found on a range of standardised measures of eating pathology including: binge eating severity; emotional overeating; external overeating; restrictive and restrained eating; dieting; and poor body image. All of these improvements were maintained at 3 months follow-up. The reduction in binge eating frequency was particularly dramatic. While 80% of women reported a binge frequency worthy of a *DSM-IV-TR* diagnosis of BN or BED at the beginning of the program, this had dropped to 14% by the 3 month follow-up.

The inclusion of a mindfulness-based component in the Mindful MEG program appears to have been particularly valuable and acceptable to the group participants. Mindfulness factors were more commonly endorsed as the "most helpful" part of the program than were CBT-factors. The drop-out rate of 12% found in the current study compares favourably to the average drop-out rate of 25% found in reviews of straight CBT programs (Shapiro et al., 2007). The qualitative data further bolsters support for the addition of mindfulness to the treatment of binge eating problems. Women attributed many of the positive changes experienced after group participation directly to mindfulness practice, including reduced binge eating frequency and severity, increased emotion regulation, and increased self-compassion. Three months after the completion of the program, over half the participants were still engaged in formal meditation, indicating that they perceived an ongoing benefit of practicing mindfulness, sufficient enough to maintain their commitment to the practice.

The main mechanisms of change through which mindfulness appeared to operate in the current study, according to the participants themselves, was through an increased level of awareness, leading to more control and choice over behaviours. Living in the present moment was also identified as a powerful tool which contributed positively to general quality of life, as was a movement from self-criticism and judgement towards self-compassion and acceptance.

## Limitations

Despite the strong results found in the current study, they should be viewed with caution due to some important limitations. The main limitation of the study was the absence of a comparison group. A control group of some form would have allowed us to compare improvements achieved in the Mindful MEG program to changes that may have occurred naturally over time, or from participation in an alternative program. Other studies have shown that BN is unlikely to improve on its own over time, and is often a chronic and unremitting disorder (Wade, Bergin, Tiggermann, Bulik, & Fairburn, 2006). The comparison of a mindfulness-based treatment program for binge eating to a traditional CBT group for binge eating would be ideal as this would generate important data on the relative effectiveness of the different treatment modes, and the unique contribution of mindfulness practices.

Participant attrition is another limitation of the study. The analyses completed in the current study were based on program completers only, and this may result in a bias of findings towards the expected hypotheses. A rudimentary attrition analysis found that women who dropped out of the program were likely to be experiencing more severe binge eating and general psychopathology, and it is possible that the pattern of attrition was not random. As such, the current findings and conclusions can only be generalised to Mindful-MEG program completers. A per protocol, or "on-treatment" analysis was considered preferable in the current study due to the small sample, and a focus on the effectiveness of the treatment program itself. Given the limitations we have identified, the findings in the current study should be considered exploratory, and a basis for future research in the area.

## Implications

Clinicians may benefit from expanding their traditional understanding of the treatment of binge eating through cognitive-behavioural therapy. The findings in the current study lend support to the preliminary but growing body of evidence supporting the value of mindfulness practice for women with binge eating problems. Mindfulness concepts and practice have the potential to add powerful additional benefits for clients, not only in regards to binge eating, but extending to broader areas of interpersonal relationships and quality of life.

Evidence is growing that tailoring mindfulness practices to the specific presenting problems will provide the most benefit to clients, though research studies specifically designed to explore this would be useful. Qualitative findings in the current study support the benefit of tailored mindfulness practices, with mindful eating identified by participants as particularly helpful in reducing binge eating frequency and severity. The development and implementation of mindfulness-based therapies using a "problem formulation" approach (Teasedale, Segal, & Williams, 2003) is highly recommended. In this approach, mindfulness interventions are customised to the problems of a specific population, with different components of mindfulness being matched with the psychopathology being targeted. For example, a mindfulness practice such as "urge surfing" is likely to be particularly useful for the treatment of addiction (Marlatt, 1994), self-compassion exercises may be well-suited for clients experiencing low self-esteem (Neff, 2003), and practices such as the body scan may be particularly helpful for clients with chronic physical pain (Kabat-Zinn, 1990).

Findings in the current study regarding the mechanisms of change through which mindfulness operates can also be of use to clinicians in their attempts to introduce mindfulness to clients, and encourage them to practice. Drawing attention to the capacity of mindfulness to promote self-awareness, increase self-compassion, and lead to greater levels of control and choice over one's behaviour may help to boost client motivation.

The continued use of qualitative research methods to understand both the outcomes of mindfulness practice, and the mechanisms of change through which it operates is recommended. The majority of studies exploring mindfulness and binge eating have utilised quantitative data, which while helpful in determining changes to outcome variables, is less able to explore the means through which mindfulness works. Mindfulness is an experiential phenomenon, and as such, is particularly suited to qualitative study (Depraz, Varela, & Vermersch, 2003).

## CONCLUSIONS

The combination of mindfulness-based treatment components with the traditional cognitive behavioural approach has the potential to provide added benefit to women experiencing binge eating problems. In the current study, participation in a combined mindfulness-CBT program led to significant reductions to binge eating frequency and severity, dieting behaviour, and body image dissatisfaction. Mindfulness-based components of the program were highly acceptable to the group participants, and identified as more helpful than the traditional CBT components. Of particular use were eating-specific mindfulness exercises, suggesting that the tailoring of mindfulness practices is a useful endeavour. Qualitative interviews reveal that mindfulness may be useful to women with binge eating difficulties through its ability to increase self-awareness, leading to more control and choice over behaviours.

# REFERENCES

American Psychiatric Association. (2000). *Diagnostic and statistical manual of mental disorders* (4th ed., text rev.). Washington, DC: Author.

Anderson, D. A., Williamson, D. A., Duchmann, E. G., Gleaves, D. H., & Barbin, J. M. (1999). Development and validation of a multifactorial treatment outcome measure for eating disorders. *Assessment, 6*(1), 7–20.

Baer, R. A., Fischer, S., & Huss, D. B. (2005). Mindfulness and acceptance in the treatment of disordered eating. *Journal of Rational-Emotive & Cognitive-Behavior Therapy, 23*, 281–300.

Baer, R. A., Smith, G. T., Hopkins, J., Krietemeyer, J., & Toney, L. (2006). Using self-report assessment methods to explore facets of mindfulness. *Assessment, 13*(1), 27–45.

Bandura, A. (1977). Self-efficacy: Towards a unifying theory of behaviour change. *Psychological Review, 84*, 191–215.

Ben-Tovim, D. I., & Walker, M. K. (1991). The development of the Ben-Tovim Walker Body Attitudes Questionnaire (BAQ), a new measure of women's attitudes towards their own bodies. *Psychological Medicine, 21*, 775–784.

Brownley, K. A., Berkman, N. D., Sedway, J. A., Lohr, K. N., & Bulik, C. M. (2007). Binge Eating Disorder treatment: A systematic review of randomized controlled trials. *International Journal of Eating Disorders, 40*, 337–348.

Carlson, L. E., Speca, M., Patel, K. D., & Goodey, E. (2003). Mindfulness-based stress reduction in relation to quality of life, mood, symptoms of stress, and immune parameters in breast and prostate cancer outpatients. *Psychosomatic Medicine, 65*, 571–581.

Clausen, L., Rosenvinge, J., Friborg, O., & Rokkedal, K. (2011). Validating the Eating Disorder Inventory-3 (EDI-3): A comparison between 561 female eating disorders patients and 878 females from the general population. *Journal of Psychopathology and Behavioral Assessment, 33*(1), 101–10.

Crafti, N. (1994). *The Moderate Eating Group (MEG): Program manual*. Melbourne, Australia: Swinburne University of Technology.

Crafti, N., & Peyton, M. (2005). *The Mindful Moderate Eating Group: A manual for the group treatment of binge eating problems*. Melbourne, Australia: Swinburne University of Technology.

Dalai Lama & Goleman, D. (2003). *Destructive emotions: How can we overcome them?* New York, NY: Bantam Books.

Depraz, N., Varela, F. J., & Vermersch, P. (2003). *On becoming aware: A pragmatics of experiencing*. Amsterdam, the Netherlands: John Benjamins.

Eldredge, K. L., Locke, K. D., & Horowitz, L. M. (1998). Patterns of interpersonal problems associated with binge eating disorder. *International Journal of Eating Disorders*, *23*, 383–389.

Fairburn, C. G., Marcus, M. D., & Wilson, G. T. (1993). Cognitive-behavioral therapy for binge eating and bulimia nervosa: A comprehensive treatment manual. In C. G. Fairburn & G. T. Wilson (Eds.), *Binge eating: Nature, assessment and treatment* (pp. 361–404). New York, NY: Guilford Press.

Feldman, G., Hayes, A., Kumar, S., Greeson, J., & Laurenceau, J.-P. (2007). Mindfulness and emotion regulation: The development and initial validation of the Cognitive and Affective Mindfulness Scale-Revised (CAMS-R). *Journal of Psychopathology and Behavior Assessment*, *29*, 177–190.

Garner, D. M. (2004). *Eating Disorders Inventory (EDI-3): Professional manual*. Lutz, FL: Psychological Assessment Resources, Inc.

Glynn, S. M., & Ruderman, A. J. (1986). The development and validation of an Eating Self-Efficacy Scale. *Cognitive Therapy and Research*, *10*, 403–420.

Hay, P., Mond, J. M., Buttner, P., & Darby, A. (2008). Eating disorder behaviours are increasing: Findings from two sequential community surveys in South Australia. *PLoS ONE*, *3*(2), e1541.

Hepworth, N. S. (2010). A mindful eating group as an adjunct to individual treatment for eating disorders: A pilot study. *Eating Disorders*, *19*, 6–16.

Isnard, P., Michel, G., Frelut, M.-L., Vila, G., Falissard, B., Naja, W., . . . Mouren-Simeoni, M.-C. (2003). Binge eating and psychopathology in severely obese adolescents. *International Journal of Eating Disorders*, *34*, 235–243.

Kabat-Zinn, J. (1990). *Full catastrophe living: How to cope with stress, pain and illness using mindfulness meditation*. New York, NY: Dell.

Kristeller, J. L., & Hallett, C. B. (1999). An exploratory study of a meditation-based intervention for binge eating disorder. *Journal of Health and Psychology*, *4*, 357–363.

Marlatt, G. A. (1994). Addiction, mindfulness, and acceptance. In S. C. Hayes, N. Jacobson, V. M. Folette, & M. J. Dougher (Eds.), *Acceptance and change: Content and context in psychotherapy* (pp. 175–197). Reno, NV: Context.

Martin, K. C., Williamson, D. A., & Thaw, J. M. (2000). Criterion validity of the Multiaxial Assessment of Eating Disorder Symptoms. *International Journal of Eating Disorders*, *28*, 303–310.

Masheb, R. M., & Grilo, C. M. (2006). Emotional overeating and its associations with eating disorder psychopathology among overweight patients with Binge Eating Disorder. *International Journal of Eating Disorders*, *39*, 141–146.

Miller, J. J., Fletcher, K., & Kabat-Zinn, J. (1995). Three-year follow-up and clinical implications of a mindfulness meditation-based stress reduction intervention in the treatment of anxiety disorders. *General Hospital Psychiatry*, *17*, 192–200.

Neff, K. (2003). Self-compassion: An alternative conceptualization of a healthy attitude toward oneself. *Self and Identity*, *2*(2), 85–101.

Roth, B., & Creaser, T. (1997). Mindfulness meditation-based stress reduction: Experience with a bilingual inner-city population. *The Nurse Practitioner*, *22*, 150–176.

Sanftner, J. L., & Crowther, J. H. (1998). Variability in self-esteem, moods, shame, and guilt in women who binge. *International Journal of Eating Disorders, 23*, 391–397.

Segal, Z. V., Williams, J. M. G., & Teasdale, J. D. (2002). *Mindfulness-based Cognitive Therapy for depression: A new approach to preventing relapse.* New York NY: Guilford Press.

Seligman, M. P. (1995). The effectiveness of psychotherapy: The Consumer Reports Study. *American Psychologist, 50*, 965–974.

Shapiro, J. R., Berkman, N. D., Brownley, K. A., Sedway, J. A., Lohr, K. N., & Bulik, C. M. (2007). Bulimia nervosa treatment: A systematic review of randomized controlled trials. *International Journal of Eating Disorders, 40*, 321–336.

Smith, J. A., & Osborn, M. (2008). Interpretative phenomenological analysis. In J. A. Smith (Ed.), *Qualitative psychology: A practical guide to research methods* (2nd ed., pp. 53–80). London, UK: Sage.

Teasdale, J. D., Segal, Z. V., & Williams, J. M. G. (2003). Mindfulness training and problem formulation. *Clinical Psychology: Science and Practice, 10*, 157–160.

van Strien, T., Engels, R. C. M. E., Van Leeuwe, J., & Snoek, H. M. (2005). The Stice model of overeating: Tests in clinical and non-clinical samples. *Appetite, 45*, 205–213.

van Strien, T., Frijters, J. E. R., Bergers, G. P. A., & Defares, P. B. (1986). The Dutch Eating Behavior Questionnaire (DEBQ) for assessment of restrained, emotional and external eating behavior. *International Journal of Eating Disorders, 5*, 295–315.

Wade, T. D., Bergin, J. L., Tiggermann, M., Bulik, C. M., & Fairburn, C. G. (2006). Prevalence and long-term course of lifetime eating disorders in an adult Australian twin cohort. *Australian and New Zealand Journal of Psychiatry, 40*, 121–128.

Wilson, G. T. (1996). Acceptance and change in the treatment of eating disorders and obesity. *Behavior Therapy, 27*, 417–439.

Yalom, I. D. (1995). *The theory and practice of group psychotherapy* (4th ed.). New York, NY: HarperCollins.

# Mindfulness-Action Based Cognitive Behavioral Therapy for Concurrent Binge Eating Disorder and Substance Use Disorders

CHRISTINE M. COURBASSON

*Eating Disorders and Addiction Clinic, Centre for Addiction and Mental Health, University of Toronto, Toronto, Ontario, Canada*

YASUNORI NISHIKAWA

*Department of Psychology, University of Toronto; and University Health Network, Toronto, Ontario, Canada*

LEAH B. SHAPIRA

*Department of Psychology, York University, Toronto, Ontario, Canada*

*Individuals with Binge Eating Disorder (BED) often evidence comorbid Substance Use Disorders (SUD), resulting in poor outcome. This study is the first to examine treatment outcome for this concurrent disordered population. In this pilot study, 38 individuals diagnosed with BED and SUD participated in a 16-week group Mindfulness-Action Based Cognitive Behavioral Therapy (MACBT). Participants significantly improved on measures of objective binge eating episodes; disordered eating attitudes; alcohol and drug addiction severity; and depression. Taken together, MACBT appears to hold promise in treating individuals with co-existing BED-SUD.*

## INTRODUCTION

Binge Eating Disorder (BED) carries significant medical complications (e.g., obesity; Williamson & Martin, 1999) as well as elevated mortality risks

---

The authors wish to thank Tamara Arenovich, Mirka Ondrack, and Maksims Volkovs for their helpful comments on this manuscript.

(Fichter, Quadflieg, & Hedlund, 2008). Likewise, Substance Use Disorders (SUD) are associated with premature death (Harris & Barraclough, 1998) and a variety of medical conditions (e.g., HIV, liver disease; Stein, 1999). Little debate exists over the strong association between BED and SUD. Indeed, lifetime prevalence rates of SUD among patients with BED have been found to be as high as 33% (Grilo, White, & Masheb, 2009; Vastag, 2001; Wilfley et al., 2000). Moreover, there is an elevated incidence of BED among diverse populations seeking treatment for SUD: individuals (Stewart, Brown, Devoulyte, Theakston, & Larsen, 2006), community samples (Javaras et al., 2008), and high school/college samples (Dunn, Larimer, & Neighbors, 2002). Given the medical and mortality risks associated with both BED and SUD, the need for effective concurrent treatment is clear. Yet no published studies have examined treatment outcomes for individuals with co-existing BED-SUD.

Patients who seek treatment for BED-SUD frequently identify themselves as having only one problem—either BED or SUD. Unfortunately, extant treatment programs and outcome trials for BED often *exclude* patients with a co-existing SUD despite the strong association between BED and SUD (Dunn et al., 2007; Wolfe & Maisto, 2000). Likewise, treatment settings for SUD typically do not formally assess for comorbid BED. As a consequence, concurrent treatment administration is prevented. Patients with both BED and SUD therefore are faced with sequentially treating their difficulties. Sequenced treatment requires sizeable time and resources, leaving patients vulnerable to increased medical risks associated with BED (Sysko & Hildebrandt, 2009). As predicted by mutual-maintenance models of mental health and substance use comorbidity (e.g., Stewart & Conrod, 2008), addressing only one problem at a time may result in an increased substitution of one maladaptive method of coping with distress (e.g., abusing substances) with another (e.g., binge eating; Courbasson, Araujo de Sorkin, Dullerud, & Van Wyk, 2007; Courbasson & Schelkanova, 2008; Varner, 1995).

An integrated model that addresses co-existing BED-SUD may be more effective, more cost-effective, and more sensitive to the idiosyncratic needs vis-à-vis such dually diagnosed patients (Courbasson et al., 2007; Sysko & Hildebrandt, 2009). Randomized clinical trials have established clinically significant effects of cognitive behavior therapy (CBT) for both BED and SUD, considered separately (Ouimette, Finney, & Moos, 1997; Wilson, Grilo, & Vitousek, 2007). However, a significant portion of participants in these treatment outcome studies do not achieve high end-state functioning at the end of treatment and at follow-up (Hamilton, Kitzman, & Guyotte, 2006; Telch, Agras, & Linehan, 2001). In an effort to improve treatment outcomes, the literature has witnessed the ascension of mindfulness training in the treatment of a wide range of psychiatric conditions including BED and SUD (see Kristeller, Baer, & Quillian-Wolever, 2006 for a review; Witkiewitz, Marlatt, & Walker, 2005).

## Binge Eating, Substance Use, and Mindfulness

A growing body of literature supports the usefulness of mindfulness-based treatments, which encourage nonjudgmental acceptance of experience, for a variety of psychiatric conditions including BED and SUD (Baer, 2003; Baer, Fischer, & Huss, 2005; Hamilton et al., 2006; Kristeller & Hallett, 1999; Smith, Shelley, Leahigh, & Vanleit, 2006; Teasdale, Segal, & Williams, 2000; Witkeiewitz et al., 2005). Cognitive interventions have included strategies designed to *challenge* or *change* the content of dysfunctional thoughts and beliefs hypothesized to play a role in the development, maintenance, and relapse of BED and SUD (Beck, Wright, & Newman, 1993; Gongora, Derksen, & van Der Staak, 2004; Kabatt-Zinn, 1982; Linehan, 1993a, b; Segal, Williams & Teasdale, 2002; Teasdale, 1999). Conversely, mindfulness-based approaches are not directed at changing the content of cognition (e.g., rational disputation), but at changing one's *attitude* toward thoughts (Baer et al., 2005; Breslin, Zack & Main, 2002). That is, mindfulness training fosters a "decentered view" of thoughts (Breslin et al., 2002; Teasdale, Segal, & Williams, 1995)—viewing them as dynamic and transient mental events, which are not necessarily grounded in fact or reality. In this vein, by fostering a meta-cognitive, observer stance on one's thoughts, mindfulness can reduce the apodicity of thoughts, ultimately contravening the urgency of behaviors (Baer et al., 2005; Breslin et al., 2002). By extension, mindfulness training may counter rigid beliefs, for example, the idea that a single lapse in a dieting rule or substance use is indicia of complete failure, thus preventing the likelihood of a full-blown relapse (e.g., "abstinence violation effect"; Marlatt, 1985).

Within a cognitive-behavioral framework, emotions are viewed as a *consequence* of cognitive change, and the etiological significance of emotions has largely been relegated to a secondary status. A more explicit focus on the role of emotions, however, may be particularly conducive in patients with co-existing BED-SUD, as recent theoretical formulations have shifted focus towards understanding binge eating and substance abuse as a failure in emotional regulation (Heatherton & Baumeister, 1991; Leahy, 2002; Stewart, 1996; Stewart et al., 2006; Wiser & Telch, 1999). To counter maladaptive emotional regulation by encouraging sustained non-judgmental, accepting observations of aversive emotions, mindfulness serves as an exposure to emotions (Baer, 2003). Such tolerance, acceptance, and conscious observation of triggers to binge eating or substance abuse should, in turn, promote greater volitional control and self-esteem, evidenced factors in the maintenance and relapse of binge eating and substance abuse (Colles, Dixon, & O'Brien, 2008; Piquero, Gibson, & Tibbetts, 2002; Proulx, 2008). Thus, incorporating mindfulness into cognitive behavioral treatments might further effectively attenuate various putative mechanisms at the core to the development and maintenance of BED and SUD.

## Current Study

This pilot study evaluated mindfulness-action based cognitive behavioral therapy (MACBT) in a sample of outpatients with co-existing BED-SUD. MACBT is an integrated treatment that draws from both mindfulness and cognitive behavioral therapies, and its features are described later in this article. To our knowledge, this study is the first to examine the clinical utility of an integrated treatment in this concurrent disordered population. We hypothesized that MACBT would lead to significant salutary effects on various maladaptive cognitive, emotional, and behavioral features associated with BED and SUD.

## METHOD

### Participants

The sample was recruited via flyers posted in a community mental health and addiction hospital, and through referrals from medical doctors, psychiatrists, and other mental health professionals at a large university affiliated mental health and addiction facility. Participants were screened via telephone prior to intake. Inclusion criteria were: (a) age 18 or older; (b) *Diagnostic and Statistical Manual of Mental Disorders, 4th ed., text revision* (*DSM-IV-TR*; American Psychiatric Association, 2000) criteria for BED and SUD, and; (c) BMI equal to or greater than 30 (or 28 with medical complications from binge eating). All participants gave written informed consent prior to entry into the study. Exclusion criteria included: (a) chronic suicidality; (b) active psychosis; (c) mental retardation, and; (d) pregnancy as this would impact weight and introduce undue variance.

Participants ($n = 38$) were primarily female ($n = 30$; male $n = 8$). The mean age of participants was 42 years ($SD = 10.96$). The majority of participants reported finishing their secondary education or a GED (76.3%), with 31% of this subset of individuals completing a four year B.A/BSc. Also, 38.46% of participants reported that they had never been married, and 33.3% were employed full time at the time of this study.

The participants' primary problematic substance was alcohol (75%) followed by cannabis (36.4%). The average age of onset of a primary substance abuse disorder was 25.6 years ($SD = 13.12$), and the majority of individuals reported dependence (70.8%) over abuse (29.2%). At baseline, participants reported an average of 5 five days for both alcohol and drug use problems in the previous month. Depression was the most frequently observed comorbid Axis I category (41%), followed by post traumatic stress disorder (33.3%). Avoidant personality disorder (20.5%) and depressive personality disorder (20.5%) were the most frequently observed Axis II disorders.

## Measures

The Structured Clinical Interview for *DSM-IV* disorders (SCID-II; First, Spitzer, Gibbon, & Williams, 1996) was used to confirm diagnoses of BED and SUD. This semi-structured diagnostic interview was administered by a trained clinician who evaluated specific criteria for the Axis I (Clinical Disorders) and Axis II (Personality Disorders) diagnoses of the *DSM-IV*. The SCID-II is widely utilized and evidences acceptable psychometric properties (First et al., 1995). Specific to eating disorders and SUD, the SCID-II has good test-retest (eating disorders: $\kappa = .64 - .84$; SUD: $\kappa = .76 - .77$) and inter-rater reliability (eating disorders; $\kappa = .73 - 1.0$; SUD: $\kappa = .95 - 1.0$; e.g., Zanarini & Frankenburg, 2001; Zanarini et al., 2000).

The Eating Disorder Examination Questionnaire (EDE-Q; Fairburn & Beglin, 1994) was used to assess the occurrence of binge eating episodes, and eating related attitudes and behaviors in the past 28 days. This 36-item self-report questionnaire is based on the Eating Disorders Examination Interview (EDE; Fairburn & Cooper, 1993) and consists of four subscales: Dietary Restraint, Eating Concern, Weight Concern, and Shape Concern. Subscale scores range from 0 to 6. The EDE-Q has demonstrated acceptable validity and reliability across the four subscales (test-retest reliability: $r = .87 - .94$, internal consistency: Cronbach $\alpha = 0.78 - 0.93$, item reliability: $\varphi$ Coefficient $= .57 - .70$; Luce & Crowther, 1999).

The Addiction Severity Index (ASI; McLellan et al., 1992), the primary outcome measure of substance use, assessed addiction severity across various areas of the client's life such as the number, extent, and duration of alcohol and substance use difficulties in the past 30 days. Participants were asked to rate the extent to which their difficulties distressed them. Composite scores on the ASI vary from 0 to 1, with higher scores indicating greater severity. The ASI is one of the most commonly used measures in research and clinical settings, with acceptable psychometric properties (test-retest reliability: $r = .83$ or above, inter-rater reliability: $r = .72 - .91$; McLellan et al., 1985; McLellan et al., 1992).

Beck Depression Inventory (BDI-II; Beck, Steer, & Brown, 1996) is a 21-item inventory used to measure the cognitive, affective, somatic, and behavioral symptoms associated with depression. This self-report measure is widely used in clinical and research settings, and has good psychometric properties (internal consistency: Cronbach $\alpha = 0.91 - 0.93$, correlation with Hamilton Depression Scale: $r = 0.71$; Beck, Steer, Ball & Ranieri, 1996; Beck et al., 1996).

## Overview of Treatment

The manualized treatment consisted of 16 weekly 2 hour group sessions. Each group was comprised of 6 to 12 male and female participants. The groups were led by two group facilitators extensively trained in concurrent eating and substance use disorders, mindfulness, and cognitive behavioral therapy. Participants were not permitted to remain in treatment if they had missed four or more consecutive group sessions, as they would have missed too much content.

To attune participants to the present and focusing inwardly, the facilitator led the group through a brief mindfulness exercise at the beginning of each session. Participants were required to engage in self-monitoring at home and complete daily practice logs pertaining to eating, emotions, and substance use. These logs were reviewed with the facilitators during the first hour of the group, exploring eating and substance use behaviors and any difficulties experienced over the past week, as well as highlighting healthy lifestyle changes. Obstacles to receiving and participating in treatment were openly discussed. The second hour of the group included the teaching of specific coping skills, physical activities, and mindfulness techniques to prevent binge eating and substance use.

## Description of Treatment

The MACBT program consisted of several components which are described below.

### MINDFULNESS

Through practice of mindfulness techniques, participants were encouraged to develop patience and trust, and to maintain an open mind. A dialectic between acceptance and change was fostered. In other words, participants were supported in not only setting realistic goals, but also accepting the reality that there were some situations which could not be changed (e.g., setting a goal of obtaining a healthy BMI and accepting that this is a healthy weight and shape for a given individual). In mindfulness practice, participants were encouraged to adopt a non-judgmental and non-striving stance. They learned to both be aware of and open to thoughts, emotions, sensations, and surroundings in the present moment.

Central to this program was teaching participants the skills to regulate emotions such as grief, anger, sadness, anxiety, happiness, and states such as boredom, *without the use of food or substances*. To this end, participants practiced how to tolerate difficult emotions and uncontrollable urges until their acuteness subsided rather than engage in maladaptive behaviors. Furthermore, participants learned to be mindful of cultural pressures that promote problematic eating and substance use such as striving for an unrealistic body shape. They were encouraged to deconstruct and challenge media messages that promote these behaviors. In addition, participants were introduced to mindfulness-based methods that could be used to recognize maladaptive antecedents to binge eating or substance use, and to prevent relapse.

## MINDFUL EATING

Participants were shown how to eat mindfully. Mindful eating included slowing down and taking time to focus entirely on the sensory qualities associated with the foods they were eating—without judgment and distractions. The goal of this practice was to prevent participants' tendency to eat mindlessly, which often can lead to consuming more food than intended as well as eating when not physically hungry.

## PSYCHOEDUCATION

Participants were provided with psychoeducation related to binge eating and substance use. Topics included the functions and commonalities between binge eating and substance use. Participants collaborated with facilitators to generate alternative healthy strategies for such behaviors. Additionally, a session was spent on nutrition education and eating hygiene. Participants were taught to examine and mindfully reframe their core beliefs related to food and substances.

## BALANCED PHYSICAL ACTIVITY

Participants learned the health risks associated with obesity, over eating, substance use, and physical inactivity. They were also taught the corresponding benefits associated with increased physical activity. Participants were expected to be physically active (within their physical capacity), starting at 5 five minutes daily in the first week, and adding an additional 5 minutes each week up to 60 minutes. They were encouraged to integrate physical activity mindfully into their everyday routine so as to create a habitually active lifestyle.

## FOCUS ON STRENGTHS

Rather than concentrating solely on treating participants' difficulties, as is found in most treatments, participants were encouraged to attend to their personal strengths. These strengths included being aware of what was going well in their lives, learning to capitalize on their existing skills, celebrating their successes over the course of treatment, engaging in positive self-talk, utilizing positive imagery, and developing compassion for themselves.

# RESULTS

## Analytic Strategy

A Generalized Linear Model was used where the dependent variable was modeled by a negative binomial distribution with log link (number of objective binge eating episodes, EDE-Q). The design was one repeated factor (time) with 2 levels (pre-treatment and post-treatment). We performed a repeated measures negative binomial analysis (RMNB) because it affords a useful alternative to Poisson regression for count data when overdispersion exists (e.g., the variance of the binge eating episodes was larger than would be expected of a true Poisson; Hausman, Hall, & Griliches, 1984). All other outcomes were analyzed using mixed model repeated measures (MMRM) analyses: disordered eating (EDE-Q), and depression (BDI). For the ASI, log transformations were performed prior to using MMRM to analyze outcome. Even while accounting for nonrandom missing data, MMRM analyses have been demonstrated to be very precise at modeling treatment outcome (e.g., Mallinckrodt, Clark, & David, 2001). Analyses were conducted using the SPSS v. 17.

## Treatment Retention

A total of 38 participants completed the baseline assessment. Of these, 29 (76.3%) completed the post-treatment assessment. The attrition rate was 23.7%, which is comparable to some of the other clinical studies of patients with BED or SUD (e.g. Marques & Formigoni, 2001; Munsch et al., 2007). Independent sample t-tests suggested no significant differences between those who completed the study compared to individuals who did not complete it based on the following variables: alcohol and drug severity (ASI), objective binge eating episodes (EDE-Q), eating disorder severity (EDE-Q), and depressive symptoms (BDI).

## Effect of Treatment–RMNB

### BINGE EATING EPISODES

Participants engaged in objective binge eating 21 times per month on average at intake ($SD = 24.05$). RMNB analyses revealed that when controlling for baseline depression scores, there was a significant reduction in the number of objective binge eating episodes over time, Wald $X^2$ (1) $= 5.82, p = .02$. Between pre- and post-treatment, MACBT participants significantly reduced the number of objective binge eating episodes reported. No significant differences over time were found for the number of days on which objective binge episodes occurred.

## Effect of Treatment–MMRM

### DISORDERED EATING

Between pre- and post-treatment, there were significant changes on the EDE-Q Eating concern scores $F(1, 19) = 10.42$, $p < .001$, EDE-Q Shape concern scores, $F(1, 19) = 9.45$, $p = .01$, EDE-Q Weight concern scores, $F(1, 19) = 5.25$, $p = .03$, and EDE-Q Global scores, $F(1, 19) = 14.11$, $p < .001$. There was a trend evidenced for the EDE-Q Restraint scores $F(1, 19) = 3.67$, $p = .07$. Participants in the MACBT group evidenced lowered concerns about shape, weight, and eating over time, and also tended to decrease in concerns related to restraint over eating.

### SUBSTANCE USE

Controlling for baseline depression scores, significant main effects were evidenced over time on the ASI-Alcohol subscale, $F(1, 28) = 4.16$, $p = .05$ and the ASI-Drug subscale, $F(1, 27) = 5.43$, $p = .03$. Participants in MACBT evidenced significantly lower scores on the drug and alcohol subscales of the ASI.

### DEPRESSION

There were significant main effects for Time on the BDI-Cognitive Affective subscale, $F(1, 27) = 19.04$, $p < .001$, the BDI-Somatic Performance Scale, $F(1, 27) = 5.13$, $p = .03$, and the BDI Total score, $F(1, 27) = 14.12$, $p < .001$. From pre- to post-treatment, depressive symptoms were reduced overall as well as specific cognitive affective and somatic performance symptoms.

## Effect Size and Power Analyses

Effect sizes were computed based on Cohen's (1988) $d$ statistic for dependent samples using G*Power 3 (see Table 1; Faul, Erdfelder, Lang, & Buchner, 2007). Per Cohen, .20, .50, and .80 were interpreted as small, medium, and large effect sizes. Large effect sizes were evidenced at the end of treatment on all outcome variables, specifically: Objective binge eating episodes, EDE-Q global and subscale scores, the ASI alcohol subscale, and BDI total and subscale scores. A medium-large effect size was present on the ASI drug subscale.

## DISCUSSION

The high prevalence of individuals presenting with comorbid mental health and substance use disorders has been widely documented (Reiger et al.,

**TABLE 1** Means, Standard Deviations, and Effect Sizes for MACBT Outcome

| Scale | Mean (SD) pre-treatment | Mean (SD) post-treatment | F | p | Effect Size |
|---|---|---|---|---|---|
| EDE-Q[a] – Objective binge eating episodes | 19.05 (4.45) | 8.09 (2.63) | 5.82* | .02 | 0.86** |
| EDE-Q – Eating concern | 3.33 (1.71) | 1.97 (1.53) | 10.42 | <.01 | 2.87 |
| EDE-Q – Shape concern | 4.17 (0.77) | 3.43 (1.29) | 9.45 | .01 | 2.31 |
| EDE-Q – Weight concern | 4.34 (0.91) | 3.62 (1.35) | 5.25 | .03 | 2.07 |
| EDE-Q – Dietary restraint | 2.05 (1.26) | 1.32 (1.35) | 3.67 | .07 | 1.89 |
| EDE-Q – Global score | 3.48 (0.85) | 2.58 (1.20) | 14.11 | <.01 | 2.85 |
| ASI[b] – Alcohol*** | 0.08 (0.07) | 0.06 (0.05) | 4.16 | .05 | 1.19 |
| ASI – Drug*** | 0.04 (0.04) | 0.03 (0.04) | 5.43 | .03 | 0.64 |
| BDI[c] – Cognitive affective | 14.33 (7.02) | 9.86 (6.04) | 19.04 | <.01 | 2.74 |
| BDI – Somatic performance | 7.81 (3.96) | 6.04 (3.79) | 5.13 | .03 | 1.84 |
| BDI – Total score | 22.14 (10.19) | 16.46 (8.96) | 14.12 | <.01 | 2.37 |

*Note.* [a]Eating Disorders Examination Questionnaire (EDE-Q; Fairburn & Beglin, 1994). [b]Addiction Severity Index (ASI; McLellan et al., 1992). [c]Beck Depression Inventory (BDI; Beck, Steer, & Brown, 1996). *Wald $X^2$ statistic reported instead of F value because of RMNB analysis. **For RMNB, effect size is equivalent to beta coefficient. ***Log transformation utilized.

1990). Such psychiatric comorbidity has been associated with increased disability, distress, and health service utilization in both community and clinical samples (Bijl, Ravelli & van Zessen, 1998; Kessler et al., 1994).

In response to the lack of studies examining effective treatments for co-existing BED-SUD, this study was conducted to examine the utility of an integrated treatment, MACBT, for this concurrent disordered population. We hypothesized that MACBT would have a positive impact on the affective and behavioral aspects of BED-SUD and reduce the attitudinal features of disordered eating.

The results of our study provided support for our predictions. Positive outcomes and large effect sizes (except for the ASI drug subscale) were evidenced on primary behavioral outcomes associated with BED and SUD. Across treatment, participants reported a significantly lower number of objective binge episodes and lower levels of alcohol and drug addiction severity even after controlling for levels of baseline depression. Because depression has been shown to exacerbate disordered eating and substance abuse (Bossert, Schmolz, Wiegand, Junker, & Krieg, 1992), it appears that there is a notable effect exerted by MACBT on specific maladaptive behaviors cardinal to BED-SUD. The reductions in both binge eating and substance use is particularly encouraging and may be due to the fact that MACBT directly addresses the functional inter-relations between BED and SUD (e.g., emotional dysregulation; Zahradnik & Stewart, 2009).

Beyond behavioral improvements, participants further reported reductions in core attitudinal features of disordered eating. Specifically, auxiliary improvements were observed on the four subscales of the EDE-Q (eating, weight, and shape concerns, and a trend for restraint concerns), lending further credence to previous findings that acceptance and present-focused approaches can ultimately lead to *changes* in cognition (Hayes, Jacobsen, Follette, & Dougher, 1994). It is plausible that the believability, significance, and meaning of such cognitions were altered indirectly through the adoption of an acceptance-based "decentered" view of thoughts.

Finally, participants demonstrated a decrease in levels of depressive symptoms (as measured by the BDI) at the end of treatment. This finding is not surprising in light of the voluminous extant literature showing the benefits of mindfulness training for depressive symptoms (Barhoefer et al., 2009; Kingston, Dooley, Bates, Lawlor & Malone, 2007; Teasdale et al., 2000) and studies showing that depression often develops as a consequence of eating pathology (Cooper & Fairburn, 1986). That depression has been shown to interfere with treatment of eating and substance use disorders (greater pre-treatment scores of depression predict greater post-treatment eating and substance use psychopathology; Bossert, Schmolz, Wiegand, Junker, & Krieg, 1992) lends further promise to the preliminary effectiveness of MACBT.

## Limitations

The current study has a few notable limitations. The lack of a control group leaves open the possibility that the findings reflect the operation of non-specific treatment effects (e.g., positive expectancies), an area that future research should address through randomized controlled trials. Also, the small sample size and lack of follow-up severely limit conclusions as to the sustainability of treatment gains.

## Conclusions and Future Directions

The current study suggests that incorporating mindfulness into traditional cognitive behavioral approaches may be promising for treating co-existing BED-SUD. Given these preliminary positive results, the next step would be to conduct a randomized control trial with a larger sample size. Additionally, future studies utilizing sophisticated designs would do well by directly comparing the differential clinical and pragmatic benefits of sequential versus integrated treatments for individuals with comorbid BED-SUD. Finally, we end by noting that greater sensitivity towards the clinical needs of patients suffering from co-existing BED-SUD within clinical practice and outcome trials are needed. Being mindful of these would do well for clinical research and practice.

# REFERENCES

American Psychiatric Association (2000). *Diagnostic and statistical manual of mental disorders* (4th ed., text rev.). Washington, DC: American Psychiatric Association.

Baer, R. A. (2003). Mindfulness training as a clinical intervention: A conceptual and empirical review. *Clinical Psychology: Science and Practice, 10*, 125–143. doi: 10.1093/clipsy/bpg015

Baer, R. A., Fischer, S., & Huss, D. B. (2005). Mindfulness-based cognitive therapy applied to binge eating: A case study. *Cognitive and Behavioral Practice, 12*, 351–358. doi:10.1016/S1077-7229(05)80057-4

Barnhofer, T., Crane, C., Hargus, E., Amarasinghe, M., Winder, R., & Williams, J. M. G. (2009). Mindfulness-based cognitive therapy as a treatment for chronic depression: a preliminary study. *Behavior Research and Therapy, 47*, 366–373. doi:10.1016/j.brat.2009.01.019

Beck, A. T., Steer, R. A., Ball, R., & Ranieri, W. F. (1996). Comparison of Beck Depression Inventories –IA and –II in psychiatric outpatients. *Journal of Personality Assessment, 67*, 588–597.

Beck, A. T, Steer, R. A., & Brown, G. K. (1996). *Manual for Beck Depression Inventory II (BDI-II)*. San Antonio, TX, Psychology Corporation.

Beck, A. T., Wright, F. D., & Newman, C. F. (1992). Cocaine abuse. In A. Freeman & F. M. Dattilio (Eds.), *Comprehensive casebook of cognitive therapy* (pp. 185–192). New York, NY: Plenum Press.

Bijl, R. V., Ravelli, A., & van Zessen, G. (1998). Prevalence of psychiatric disorder in the general population: Results of the Netherlands Mental Health Survey and Incidence Study (NEMESIS). *Social Psychiatry and Psychiatric Epidemiology, 33*, 587–595. doi: 10.1007/s001270050098

Bossert, S., Schmölz, U., Wiegand, M., Junker, M., & Krieg, J. C. (1992). Predictors of short-term treatment outcome in bulimia nervosa inpatients. *Behavior Research and Therapy, 30*, 193–199.

Breslin, F. C., Zack, M., & McMain, S. (2002). An information-processing analysis of mindfulness: Implications for relapse prevention in the treatment of substance abuse. *Clinical Psychology: Science and Practice, 9*, 275–299. doi: 10.1093/clipsy/9.3.275

Cohen, J. (1988). *Statistical power analysis for the behavioural sciences* (2nd ed.). Hillsdale, NJ: Erlbaum.

Colles, S. L., Dixon, J. B., & O'Brien, P. E. (2008). Loss of control is central to psychological disturbance associated with binge eating disorder. *Obesity, 16*, 608–614. doi: 10.1038/oby.2007.99

Cooper, P. J., & Fairburn, C. G. (1986). The depressive symptoms of bulimia nervosa. *British Journal of Psychiatry, 148*, 268–274. doi: 10.1192/bjp.148.3.268

Courbasson, C. M. A., Araujo de Sorkin, A., Dullerud, B., & Van Wyk, L. (2007). Acupuncture treatment for women with concurrent substance use and anxiety/depression: An effective alternative therapy? *Family and Community Health, 30*, 112–120. doi:10.1097/01.FCH.0000264408.36013.03

Courbasson, C. M. A., & Schelkanova, I. (2008). Women and addictions: Body weight and shape concerns as barriers to recovery from substance use disorders. Let's address these issues in treatment and recovery now! *Journal of Drug Addiction, Education, and Eradication, 4,* 203–216.

Dunn, E. C., Geller, J., Neighbors, C., Brown, K. E., Williams, K. D., & Jones, M. I. (2007, November). *Women with severe eating disorders and concurrent substance use disorders: Prevalence and barriers to treatment.* Poster presented at the 41st annual conference of the Association for Behavioural and Cognitive Therapies, Philadelphia, PA.

Dunn, E. C., Larimer, M. E., & Neighbors, C. (2002). Alcohol and drug-related negative consequences in college students with bulimia nervosa and binge eating disorder. *International Journal of Eating Disorders, 32*, 171–178. doi: 10.1002/eat.10075.

Fairburn, C. G., & Beglin, S. J. (1994). Assessment of eating disorders: Interview or self-report questionnaire? *International Journal of Eating Disorders, 16*, 363–370.

Fairburn, C. G., & Cooper, Z. (1993). The eating disorder examination. In C. G. Fairburn & G. T. Wilson (Eds.), *Binge eating: Nature, assessment and treatment* (12th ed.; pp. 317–360). New York, NY: Guilford Press.

Faul, F., Erdfelder, E., Lang, A. G., & Buchner, A. (2007). G*Power 3: A flexible statistical power analysis program for the social, behavioural, and biomedical sciences. *Behavior Research Methods, 39(2)*, 175–191.

Fichter, M. M., Quadflieg, N., & Hedlund, S. (2008). Long-term course of binge eating disorder and bulimia nervosa: Relevance for nosology and diagnostic criteria. *International Journal of Eating Disorders, 41*, 577–586. doi: 10.1002/eat.20539

First, M. B., Spitzer, R. L., Gibbon, M., & Williams, J. B. W. (1995). *Structured clinical interview for DSM-IV Axis I Disorders (SCID-IP).* Washington, DC: American Psychiatry Press.

Gongora, V. C., Derksen, J. J., & van Der Staak, C. P. F. (2004). The role of specific core beliefs in the specific cognitions of bulimic patients. *Journal of Nervous and Mental Disease, 192*, 297–303. doi: 10.1097/01.nmd.0000120889.01611.2f 10.1016/j.drugalcdep.2006.05.012

Grilo, C. M., White, M. A., & Masheb, R. M. (2009). DSM-IV psychiatric disorder comorbidity and its correlates in binge eating disorder. *International Journal of Eating Disorders, 42*, 228–234. doi: 10.1002/eat.20599

Hamilton, N. A., Kitzman, H., & Guyotte, S. (2006). Enhancing health and emotion: Mindfulness as a missing link between cognitive therapy and positive psychology. *Journal of Cognitive Psychotherapy. Special Issue: Positive Psychology, 20*, 123–134. doi: 10.1891/jcop.20.2.123

Harris, E. C., & Baraclough, B. (1998). Excess mortality of mental disorder. *British Journal of Psychiatry, 173*, 11–53.

Hausman, J., Hall, B. H., & Griliches, Z. (1984). Econometric models for count data with an application to the patents—R & D relationship. *Econometrica, 52*, 909–938.

Hayes, S. C., Jacobson, N. S., Follette, V. M., & Dougher, M. J. (Eds.). (1994). *Acceptance and change: Content and context in psychotherapy.* Reno, NV: Context Press.

Heatherton, T. F., & Baumeister, R. F. (1991). Binge eating as an escape from self-awareness. *Psychological Bulletin, 110,* 86–108. doi:10.1037/0033-2909.110.1.86

Javaras, K. N., Pope, H. G., Jr., Lalonde, J. K., Roberts, J. L., Nillni, Y. I., Laird, N. M., . . . Rosenthal, N.R. (2008). Co-occurrence of binge eating disorder with psychiatric and medical disorders. *Journal of Clinical Psychiatry, 69,* 266–273.

Kabat-Zinn, J. (1982). An outpatient program in behavioural medicine for chronic pain patients based on the practice of mindfulness meditation: Theoretical considerations and preliminary results. *General Hospital Psychiatry, 4,* 33–47. doi:10.1016/0163-8343(82)90026-33

Kessler, R. C., McGonagle, K. A., Zhao, S., Nelson, C. B., Hughes, M., Eshleman, S., . . . Kendler, K.S. (1994). Lifetime and 12-month prevalence of DSM-III-R psychiatric disorders in the United States. Results from the National Comorbidity Survey. *Archives of General Psychiatry, 51,* 8–19.

Kingston, T., Dooley, B., Bates, A., Lawlor, E., & Malone, K. (2007). Mindfulness-based cognitive therapy for residual depressive symptoms. *British Psychological Society, 80,* 193–203. doi: 10.1348/147608306X116016

Kristeller, J. L., Baer, R. A., & Quillian-Wolever, R. (2006). Mindfulness-based approaches to eating disorders. In R. Baer (Ed.), *Mindfulness-based treatment approaches: Clinician's guide to evidence base and applications.* (pp. 75–91). San Diego, CA: Elsevier Academic Press.

Kristeller, J. L., & Hallett, C. B. (1999). An exploratory study of a meditation-based intervention for binge eating disorder. *Journal of Health Psychology, 4,* 357–363. doi: 10.1177/135910539900400305

Leahy, R. L. (2002). A model of emotional schemas. *Cognitive and Behavioural Practice, 9,* 177–171. doi:10.1016/S1077-7229(02)80048-7

Linehan, M. M. (1993a). *Cognitive-behavioural treatment of borderline personality disorder.* New York, NY: Guilford Press.

Linehan, M. M. (1993b). *Skills training manual for treating borderline personality disorder.* New York, NY: Guilford Press.

Luce, K. H., & Crowther, J. H. (1999). The reliability of the Eating Disorder Examination-Self Report Questionnaire version (EDE-Q). *International Journal of Eating Disorders, 25,* 349–351. doi: 10.1002/(SICI)1098-108X(199904)25: 33.0.CO;2-M

Mallinckrodt, C. H., Clark, W. S., & David, S. R. (2001). Accounting for dropout bias using mixed effects models. *Journal of Biopharmaceutical Statistics, 11,* 9–21. doi: 10.1081/BIP-100104194

Marlatt, G. A. (1985). Controlled drinking: The controversy rages on. *American Psychologist, 40,* 374–375. doi: 10.1037/0003-066X.40.3.374

Marques, A. C. P. R., & Formigoni, M. L. O. S. (2001). Comparison of individual and group cognitive-behavioral therapy for alcohol and/or drug dependent patients. *Addiction, 96,* 835–846. Doi:10.1046/j.1360-0443.2001.9668355.x

McLellan, A. T., Kushner, H., Metzger, D., Peters, R., Smith, I., Grisson, G., & Pettinati, H. (1992). The fifth edition of the Addiction Severity Index: Historical critique and normative data. *Journal of Substance Abuse Treatment, 9*, 199–213. doi: 10.1016/0740-5472(92)90062-S

McLellan, A. T., Luborsky, L., Cacciola, J., Griffith, J., Evans, F., . . . O' Brien, C. P. (1985). New data from the Addiction Severity Index: Reliability and validity in three centres. *Journal of Nervous and Mental Disease, 173*, 412–423.

Munsch, S., Biedert, E., Meyer, A., Michael, T., Schlup, B., Tuch, A., & Margraf, J. (2007). A randomised comparison of cognitive behavioral therapy and behavioral weight loss treatment for overweight individuals with binge eating disorder. *International Journal of Eating Disorders, 40*, 102–113. doi: 10.1002/eat.20350

Ouimette, P. C., Finney, J. W., & Moos, R. H. (1997). Twelve step and cognitive-behavioral treatment for substance abuse: A comparison of treatment effectiveness. *Journal of Consulting and Clinical Psychology, 65*, 230–240. doi: 10.1037/0022-006X.65.2.230

Piquero, A. R., Gibson, C. L., & Tibbetts, S. G. (2002). Does self-control account for the relationship between binge drinking and alcohol-related behaviours? *Criminal Behaviour and Mental Health, 12*, 135–154. doi: 10.1002/cbm.492

Proulx, K. (2008). Experiences of women with bulimia nervosa in a mindfulness-based eating disorder treatment group. *Eating Disorders: The Journal of Treatment & Prevention, 16*, 52–72. doi: 10.1080/10640260701773496

Reiger, D. A., Farmer, M. E., Rae, D. S., Locke, B. Z., Keith, S. J., Judd, L. L., & Goodwin, F. K. (1990). Co-morbidity of mental disorders with alcohol and other drug abuse: Results from the Epidemiological Catchment Area (ECA) study. *Journal of the American Medical Association, 264*, 2511–2518.

Segal, Z. V., Williams, J. M. G., & Teasdale, J. D. (2002). *Mindfulness-based cognitive therapy for depression: A new approach to preventing relapse*. New York, NY: Guilford Press.

Smith, B. W., Shelley, B. M., Leahigh, L., & Vanleit, B. (2006). A preliminary study of the effects of a modified mindfulness intervention on binge eating. *Complementary Health Practice Review, 11*, 133–143.

Stein, M. D. (1999). Medical consequences of substance abuse. *Psychiatric Clinics of North America, 22*, 351–370.

Stewart, S. H. (1996). Alcohol abuse in individuals exposed to trauma: A critical review. *Psychological Bulletin, 120*, 83–112. doi:10.1037/0033-2909.120.1.83

Stewart, S. H., Brown, C. G., Devoulyte, K., Theakston, J., & Larsen, S. E. (2006). Why do women with alcohol problems binge eat? Exploring connections between binge eating and heavy drinking in women receiving treatment for alcohol problems. *Journal of Health Psychology, 11*, 409–425. doi:10.1177/1359105306063313

Stewart, S. H., & Conrod, P. J. (2008). Anxiety disorder and substance use disorder co-morbidity: Common themes and future directions. In S. H. Stewart & P. J. Conrod (Eds.), *Anxiety and substance use disorders* (pp. 239–257). New York, NY: Springer.

Sysko, R., & Hildebrandt, T. (2009). Cognitive-behavioural therapy for individuals with bulimia nervosa and a co-occurring substance use disorder. *European Eating Disorders Review, 17*, 89–100. doi: 10.1002/erv.906.

Teasdale, J. D. (1999). Emotional processing, three modes of mind and the prevention of relapse in depression. *Behaviour Research and Therapy. Special Issue: Cognitive Behaviour Therapy: Evolution and prospects. A festschrift in honour of Dr S. Rachman, Editor of Behavior Research and Therapy, 37*(Suppl 1), S53–S77. doi: 10.1016/S0005-7967(99)00050-9

Teasdale, J. D., Segal, Z., & Williams, J. M. G. (1995). How does cognitive therapy prevent depressive relapse and why should attentional control (mindfulness) training help? *Behaviour Research and Therapy, 33*(1), 25–39. doi: 10.1016/0005-7967(94)E0011-7

Teasdale, K. D., Segal, Z. V., Williams, J. M. G., Ridgeway, V. A., Soulsby, J. M., & Lau, M. A. (2000). Prevention of relapse/recurrence in major depression by mindfulness-based cognitive therapy. *Journal of Consulting and Clinical Psychology, 68*, 615–623. doi: 10.1037/0022-006X.68.4.615

Telch, C. F., Agras, W. S., & Linehan, M. M. (2001). Dialectical behavior therapy for binge eating disorder. *Journal of Consulting and Clinical Psychology, 69*, 1061–1065. doi: 10.1037/0022-006X.69.6.1061

Varner, L. (1995). Dual diagnosis: Patients with eating and substance related disorders. *Journal of the American Dietetic Association, 95*, 224–225. doi: 10.1016/S0002-8223(95)00052-6

Vastag, B. (2001). What's the connection? No easy answers for people with eating disorders and drug abuse. *Journal of the American Medical Association, 285*, 1006–1007. doi:10.1001/jama.285.8.1006

Wilfley, D. E., Friedman, M. A., Dounchis, J. Z., Stein, R. I., Welch, R. R., & Ball, S. A. (2000). Comorbid psychopathology in binge eating disorder: Relation to eating disorder severity at baseline and following treatment. *Journal of Consulting and Clinical Psychology, 68*, 641–649. doi: 10.I037/TO22-006X.68.4641

Williamson, D. A., & Martin, C. K. (1999). Binge eating disorder: A review of the literature after publication of DSM-IV. *Eating and Weight Disorders, 4*, 103–114.

Wilson, G. T., Grilo, C. M., & Vitousek, K. M. (2007). Psychological treatment of eating disorders. *American Psychologist, 62*, 199–216. doi: 10.1037/0003-066X.62.3.199

Wilson, G. T., Loeb, K. L., Walsh, B. T., Labouvie, E., Petkova, E., LIU,. X., & Waternaux, C. (1999). Psychological versus pharmacological treatments of bulimia nervosa: predictors and processes of change. *Journal of Consulting and Clinical Psychology, 67*, 451–459. doi: 10.1037/0022-006X.67.4.451

Wiser, S., & Telch, C. F. (1999). Dialectical behavior therapy for binge-eating disorder. *Journal of Clinical Psychology, 55*, 755–768. doi: 10.1002/(SICI)1097-4679(199906)55:63.0.CO;2-R

Witkiewitz, K., Marlatt, G. A., & Walker, D. D. (2005). Mindfulness-based relapse prevention for alcohol use disorders: The meditative tortoise wins the race. *Journal of Cognitive Psychotherapy, 19*, 221–228. doi: 10.1037/0893-164X.20.3.343

Wolfe, W. L., & Maisto, S. A. (2000). Eating disorders and substance use: Moving beyond co-prevalence research. *Clinical Psychology Review, 20*, 617–631. doi: 10.1016/S0272-7358(99)00009-4

Zahradnik, M., & Stewart, S. (2009). Anxiety disorders and substance use disorder comorbidity: Epidemiology, theories of interrelation, and recent treatment approaches. In M. Antony & M. Stein (Eds.), *Handbook of anxiety and the anxiety disorders* (pp. 565–575). Oxford, UK: Oxford University Press.

Zanarini, M. C., & Frankenburg, F. R. (2001). Attainment and maintenance of reliability of axis I and axis II disorders over the course of a longitudinal study. *Comprehensive Psychiatry, 42*, 369–374.

Zanarini, M. C., Skodol, A. E., Bender, D., Dolan, R., Sanislow, C., Schaefer, E., . . . . Gunderson, M.D. (2000). The collaborative longitudinal personality disorders study: Reliability of axis I and II diagnoses. *Journal of Personal Disorders, 14*, 291–299.

# The Application of Mindfulness to Eating Disorders Treatment: A Systematic Review

ROCÍO GUARDIOLA WANDEN-BERGHE

*Departments of Community Nursing, Preventive Medicine, and Public Health and History of Science, University of Alicante, Alicante, Spain*

JAVIER SANZ-VALERO

*Departments of Community Nursing, Preventive Medicine, and Public Health and History of Science, University of Alicante; and Department of Public Health, History of Science, and Gynaecology, Miguel Hernández University, Alicante, Spain*

CARMINA WANDEN-BERGHE

*Department of Physiology, Pharmacology and Toxicology, University Cardenal Herrera-CEU, Elche, Spain*

*The present study is an exploratory examination of the efficacy of the application of mindfulness-based interventions to the treatment of eating disorders. It employs a systematic review technique in which terms from the Psychological Index Terms of the American Psychological Association (APA) were chosen and analyzed in conjunction with Boolean operators. Using data obtained by the online consultation of references from 12 different bibliographical databases, 8 studies were included in the systematic review. Each study reported satisfactory results, although trial qualities were variable and sample sizes were small. Nonetheless, the current study found initial evidence supporting the effectiveness of mindfulness-based interventions to the treatment of eating disorders. The application of mindfulness-based interventions to the*

We are grateful to the reviewers for their contributions. They were useful in summarizing and improving this paper.

*treatment of eating disorders remains a promising approach worthy of further research.*


# INTRODUCTION

Mindfulness is recognized as a relevant component of the various third generation behavioral therapies, including Acceptance and Commitment Therapy (ACT), Dialectical Behavior Therapy (DBT) and Mindfulness-based Cognitive Therapy (MBCT; Vallejo, 2006). Mindfulness initially was applied to alternative physiological and emotional procedures, but increasingly it has been applied to conventional psychotherapeutic approaches as well. These more recent applications have been supported by the publication of research establishing the benefit of mindfulness-based approaches to the treatment of physiological disorders such as: chronic pain (Elomaa, de C Williams & Kalso, 2009), fibromyalgia (Lush, Salmon, Floyd, Studts, Weissbecker & Sephton, 2009), and chronic fatigue syndrome (Surawy, Roberts & Silver, 2005). Further support has been shown by the publication of current research regarding the efficacy of mindfulness-based interventions to the treatment of psychological disorders as well, such as: sleep disorders (Ong, Shapiro & Manber, 2008), anxiety disorders (Davis, Strasburger & Brown, 2007), addictions (Hsu, Grow & Marlatt, 2008), and several other psychopathologies (Gaylord et al., 2009; Ledesma & Kumano, 2009).

Moreover, there is emerging evidence of its utility in the treatment of eating disorders (Corstorphine, 2006). Lavander, Jardin, and Anderson (2009) found that non-eating disordered individuals who exhibited higher levels of dispositional mindfulness were less likely to engage in disordered eating behaviors. Other research suggests that mindfulness-based skills offered to young women earlier in their psychosocial development might assist in the prevention of eating disorders (Proulx, 2008). Mindfulness-based interventions, in combination with the development of emotion regulation and distress tolerance skills, also have proven effective in the management of the urge to binge eat when it arises (Leahey, Crowther, & Irwin, 2008). There is now a burgeoning interest in the application of mindfulness as a treatment for specific categories of eating disorders, such as anorexia nervosa (Heffner, Sperry, Eifert, & Detweiler, 2002), bulimia nervosa (Safer, Telch, & Agras, 2001), and binge eating (Safer, Lock, & Couturier, 2007). Although mindfulness-based approaches are increasingly being used to treat eating disorders, empirical evidence regarding their effectiveness has not been established. The objective of this study was to provide an exploratory examination of the empirical basis for mindfulness-based interventions in the treatment of patients with eating disorders.

# METHOD

## Study Design

A literature search on the application of mindfulness-based approaches to the treatment of eating disorders was conducted. Articles obtained were analyzed using the systematic review technique.

## Literature Search

Following an examination of the Psychological Index Terms of the American Psychological Association (APA), the terms "Eating Disorders" (including the dependent Descriptors *Anorexia Nervosa, Bulimia Nervosa,* and *Binge Eating Disorder*), "Mindfulness," "Acceptance and Commitment Therapy," "Dialectical Behavior Therapy," and "Mindfulness-based Cognitive Therapy" were chosen and used in conjunction with Boolean operators: "Eating Disorders" AND ("Mindfulness" OR "Acceptance and Commitment Therapy" OR "Dialectical Behavior Therapy" OR "Mindfulness-based Cognitive Therapy"). The final equation was adapted to each bibliographic database consulted. No limit was used.

The search was carried out from the earliest date possible (according to each database) until January 2010, the latest date considered in the present study.

## Sources for the Collection of Data

The data were obtained by online consultation of the references from the following bibliographical databases: MEDLINE (via PubMed), Psychology Information (PsycINFO), Psychology Documents (PSICODOC), EMBASE, Cochrane Library, the Institute for Scientific Information (ISI) Web of Science, Food Science & Technology Abstracts (FSTA), International Pharmaceutical Abstracts (IPA), the Sociological Abstracts, Latin American and Caribbean Health Sciences Literature (LILACS), Spanish Health Sciences Bibliographic Index (IBECS), and the Spanish Medical Index (IME). Additionally, as a secondary search, the bibliographies given in the selected articles were reviewed in order to identify studies not found by the primary search.

## Selection of the Articles

The studies were evaluated independently by two of the authors of the present review (RGWB and CWB). The third author (JSV) resolved any divergences of opinion, with an observed agreement rate of 94%. Quality control of the information was carried out using double entry tables and the errors detected were corrected by consulting the originals. Subsequently, the studies were grouped with the objective of systematizing and facilitating an understanding of all the reviewed articles' findings.

Inclusion criteria for the study were twofold: a) original articles published in peer-reviewed journals, and b) studies where mindfulness has been used as therapy for eating disorders. Exclusion criteria were articles where patients with eating disorders had been diagnosed with co-morbidities that might interfere with treatment, such as severe acute mood disorders, psychosis, personality disorders and substance abuse. No articles were rejected because of methodological limitations. No restrictions were made as to the gender of participants, the age, or the type of sample.

## Data Extraction

All the relevant data, including measures of obsolescence and the Price index (percentage of references equal to or less than 5 years old), were extracted from each paper. Specifically, we extrapolated the following fields into a data extraction table: authors and year of publication, study design, type of therapy, sample (population treated) and mean age, follow-up period, diagnosis, treatment overview, and treatment components.

## RESULTS

A total of 64 articles were found, of which 10 (15.63%) were obtained from MEDLINE; 27 (42.19%) from PsycINFO; 15 (23.44%) from EMBASE; 6 (9.38%) from ISI Web of Knowledge; 4 (6.25%) from Scopus; 1 (1.56%) from FSTA, and; 1 (1.56%) from the Sociological Abstracts. No articles were obtained from the Cochrane Library, PSICODOC, LILACS, IPA, IBECS and IME. 14 (21.88%) repeated articles were found and 21 (32.81%) were not original articles; leaving 30 documents which were valid for the study. Only a total of 8 papers fulfilled all the pre-established criteria and were finally included in the systematic review. All of them were written in English. A detailed map of the selection procedure is shown in Figure 1.

The mean age of the articles was $4.50 \pm 1.21$ years (CI 95% 1.64–7.36), with a minimum of 1 and maximum of 10 years. The obsolescence of the articles examined, measured by the Median, was 3.50 years and the Price index was 62.50% (percentage of references equal to or less than 5 years old).

## Article Characteristics

Table 1 summarizes the most relevant characteristics of the articles included in the present study, such as the: study design, therapy utilized, population treated, follow-up period, and main conclusions. All of the articles included

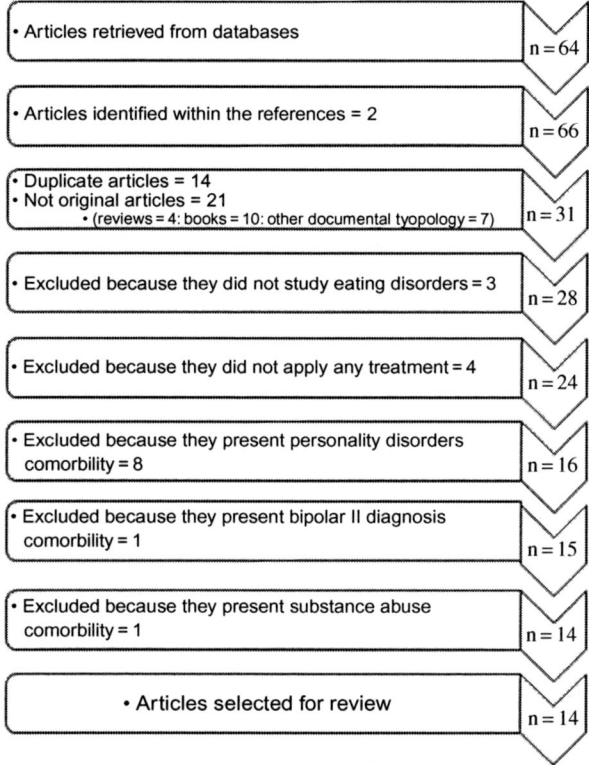

**FIGURE 1** Flowchart for article selection.

in the current study used a prospective design for the question under examination. The disparity of the articless can be seen in the wide diversity of the follow-up periods (from 3 weeks up to 6 months; in 3 studies [37.50%] this period was not stated).

Only 1 article included males, so females comprised the majority of the total samples (36 patients in the aggregate of all the studies). The number of patients treated in each article varied widely, from a minimum of 1 (in 5 studies, 62.50%) to a maximum of 18 (in 1 study, 12.50%). Patients' mean age was also very different, ranging from 15 to 54 years.

The ethnicity of the participants was reported in 4 (50.00%) out of 8 studies and the majority ethnic group was Caucasian.

## Applied Therapy

The articles included the third-generation therapies listed in the introduction of this review, although 4 of them (50.00%) used adaptations; integrating elements from MBSR or DBT and/or CBT with guided eating meditations.

**TABLE 1** Summary of Articles Reviewed Regarding the Study Characteristics and Main Conclusions in the Mindfulness Application for Eating Disorders Treatment, in Chronological Order.

| Reference | Study design | Therapy | Population treated | Follow-up period | Main conclusions |
|---|---|---|---|---|---|
| 1. Leahey et al. (2008) | Prospective | Cognitive-Behavioral mindfulness intervention. (CBMI) | $N = 7$ Gender: 6 F/1M Age: Mean 54 Ethnic group: 1 African American/ 6 Caucasian | Is not stated | Group members not only reported reductions in binge eating and eating in response to emotions, they also reported decreased eating concern, increased eating self-efficacy and improvements in emotion regulation. |
| 2. Proulx (2008) | Prospective | Mindfulness based intervention. (MBI) | $N = 6$ Gender: F Age: College-age Ethnic group: Is not stated | Is not stated | There is great potential for helping women recover from bulimia nervosa in the context of a structured, experiential, M-BED group. It provides a powerful intervention to build self-awareness, interpersonal connection, and positive coping skills, while reducing intense emotional reactivity, judgmental thoughts, and self-harming behaviors. |
| 3. Safer et al. (2007) | Prospective | Dialectical Behavior Therapy (DBT) | $N = 1$ Gender: F Age: 16 Diagnosis: Binge Eating Ethnic group: Is not stated | 3 months | DBT is acceptable, feasible, and effective for this younger population. In addition to decreasing her binge eating by the end of treatment and generally maintaining these improvements at follow-up. |

(*Continued*)

**TABLE 1** (*Continued*)

| Reference | Study design | Therapy | Population treated | Follow-up period | Main conclusions |
|---|---|---|---|---|---|
| 4. Corstorphine (2006) | Prospective | Cognitive-Emotional-Behavioral Therapy (CEBT) | $N = 1$<br>Gender: F<br>Age: 22<br>Ethnic group: Is not stated | Is not stated | This therapy reconfigures existing material in a format that has the potential to reduce the frequency and severity of impulsive behaviours, including eating-disordered behaviours. |
| 5. Baer et al. (2005) | Prospective | Mindfulness-based cognitive therapy (MBCT) | $N = 1$<br>Gender: F<br>Age: mid 50's<br>Ethnic group: Caucasian | 6 months | Substantial improvements in symptoms and preliminary evidence of increases in mindfulness.<br>Unexpected outcomes: increase in subjective binges (although this fell to zero by 6 months follow-up) and increases in restraint and weight concern. |
| 6. Heffner et al. (2002) | Prospective | Acceptance and Commitment therapy. | $N = 1$<br>Gender: F<br>Age: 15<br>BMI: 17.54<br>Ethnic group: Caucasian. | 4 monthly sessions | The patient's weight increased to a healthy level of 56.7 kg at termination, her desire for thinness and feelings of ineffectiveness decreased, and her menstrual cycle returned. Treatment gains were maintained at the follow-up. |

| | | | | | |
|---|---|---|---|---|---|
| 7. Safer et al. (2001) | Prospective | Dialectical Behavior therapy (DBT) | $N = 1$<br>Gender: F<br>Edad: 36<br>Ethnic group: Caucasian | 3 and 6 months | Positive results and rather than using food to help her manage her emotions, the therapy had taught her to identify her emotions and subsequently to utilize skills she had learned, such as diaphragmatic breathing, mindful eating, and radical acceptance. |
| 8. Kristeller et al. (1999) | Prospective | Mindfulness based intervention | $N = 21 - 3 = 18$<br>Gender: F<br>Age: Mean 46.5 years ($SD$ 5 10.5), with a range from 25 to 62<br>Ethnic group: Is not stated | 3 weeks | Substantial changes in behavior and emotional state were observed In particular, the number of reported binges, their intensity, and attitudes toward eating. Participants also reported a significant improvement in a sense of mindfulness, perceived control of eating, and awareness of hunger and satiety. |

As seen in Table 2, the eating disorder diagnosis in 4 (50%) of the articles was Binge Eating Disorder. In 3 (37.5%), the diagnosis was Bulimia Nervosa. Only 1 (12.5%) article involved patients with anorexia nervosa. It is important to mention that the difference in the Treatment Overview sections reflected differences in the type of therapy used. Studies using MBCT were typically of shorter duration than studies using DBT or ACT. Regarding the Treatment Components, it was found that these varied depending on the type of therapy and treatment population concerned. In addition, the articles used a variety of different Mindfulness techniques including Body scan, Mini-meditations or Mindful Stretching and Walking Meditation.

# DISCUSSION

Recent years have witnessed a growing interest in the application of mindfulness-based interventions as a treatment for eating disorders, ranging from anorexia nervosa (Heffner et al., 2002) and bulimia nervosa (Safer et al., 2001) to binge eating (Safer et al., 2007). Although the application of mindfulness-based treatments is growing, empirical evidence regarding its efficacy has not been established. The objective of this study was to provide an exploratory examination of the empirical basis for mindfulness-based interventions in the treatment of patients with eating disorders. The results of our study's systemic review indicate that mindfulness-based therapies may be effective in the treatment of eating disorders. Although trial qualities were variable and sample sizes were small, it is noteworthy that all of the articles that met this study's criterion reported statistically positive outcomes. Positive outcomes were observed for bulimia nervosa, anorexia nervosa, and binge eating disorder. Moreover, a variety of mindfulness-based interventions were applied, suggesting that a variety of these techniques may be utilized with satisfactory results in the treatment of eating disorders.

The validity of the articles selected for this descriptive study must be emphasized. Validity was confirmed by both the measure of obsolescence and by high scores on the Price index. Although several studies addressed broader health issues, similar results have also been obtained in the field of Psychology (Barrios, Borrego, Vilaginés, Ollé, & Somoza, 2008; Hart, 2007).

## Limitations

The present study has several limitations which are not surprising given its exploratory nature. The review reveals the lack of homogeneity of the reviewed studies. Studies used different adaptations of mindfulness therapies, treated different patient and diagnostic populations, and had variable sample sizes. There were also significant differences in methodology and

**TABLE 2** Summary of the Articles Reviewed Regarding the Therapies Used in the Mindfulness Application for Eating Disorders Treatment, in Chronological Order

| Reference | Diagnosis | Therapy | Treatment overview | Treatment components |
|---|---|---|---|---|
| Leahey et al. (2008) | Binge eating | Cognitive-Behavioral mindfulness intervention (CBMI) | Group intervention 75 min. once a week for 10 weeks | Psychoeducation. Controlling the diet and external triggers. Change problematic thought processes, increase mindfulness practices and improve coping skills. Solidifying newly learned behavior, ways of thinking, mindfulness techniques, and emotion-regulation strategies. |
| Proulx (2008) | Bulimia nervosa | Mindfulness based intervention (MBI) | Group intervention for 8 weeks | Experiential meditation practice. Psychoeducation. Discussion and assigned home practice (body scan or sitting meditation). |
| Safer et al. (2007) | Binge eating | Dialectical Behavior Therapy (DBT) | 21-60 min. individual sessions, with some of these being expanded to family sessions (for an additional 30 to 60 min.) as needed | Orientation to the DBT Model for binge eating. Distress tolerance skills, mindfulness skills. Emotion regulation skills. Interpersonal effectiveness skills. Modifications for adolescents such as family sessions. |

*(Continued)*

**TABLE 2** (*Continued*)

| Reference | Diagnosis | Therapy | Treatment overview | Treatment components |
|-----------|-----------|---------|--------------------|----------------------|
| Corstorphine (2006) | Bulimia nervosa | Cognitive-Emotional-Behavioral Therapy (CEBT) | Individual sessions | Psychoeducation. Techniques to enhance emotion and motivation to change. Experiential exercises. Strategies to restructure beliefs about the experience and expression of emotions. Identifying and responding to primary emotions adaptively. |
| Baer et al. (2005) | Binge eating | Mindfulness-based cognitive therapy (MBCT) | 10 sessions programme with 2 hour weekly sessions | Body scan. Mindful stretching and walking. Sitting meditation. Generalization of mindfulness to daily life. Cognitive therapy elements. Homework including daily practice of mindfulness exercises. |
| Heffner et al. (2002) | Anorexia nervosa, restricting type | Acceptance and Commitment therapy (ACT) | 14 sessions | Creative hopelessness. Control is the problem. Self as context. Choosing a valued direction. Letting go of struggle/embracing symptoms. Behavior change commitment.* (All by means of ACT metaphors) |

(*Continued*)

**TABLE 2** *(Continued)*

| Reference | Diagnosis | Therapy | Treatment overview | Treatment components |
|---|---|---|---|---|
| Safer et al. (2001) | Bulimia nervosa | Dialectical Behavior therapy (DBT) | 20 sessions of weekly 50 min. individual psychotherapy | Teaching emotional regulation skills. Core mindfulness. Emotion regulation and distress tolerance. Review of skills. Planning for the future. |
| Kristeller et al. (1999) | Binge eating | Mindfulness based intervention (MBI) | Groups from 3 to 9 participants, 7 sessions 6 weeks | General mindfulness meditation. Eating meditation. Mini-meditations. Homework included daily meditation and mindful-eating exercises. |

follow-up times. This variability precludes meaningful meta-analysis, thus making direct comparison awkward, especially with those studies that applied non-controlled treatments.

The treatments applied in the studies on bulimia nervosa and binge eating were based on DBT or MBCT. The results for all of them were satisfactory. However, MBCT is considerably briefer than DBT, so it is important to pursue this line of investigation in order to ascertain which of the two therapies is the most efficient and effective for these disorders.

In addition, although DBT includes mindfulness training, this is much less intensive than in MBCT, which encourages at least 45 minutes of daily mindfulness practice. Similarly, although the ACT approach to anorexia described by Heffner et al. (2002) included mindful awareness and non-judgmental acceptance of internal experience, it also included explicit encouragement of behavior changes consistent with valued goals, as well as other cognitive-behavioral change strategies, and did not include formal mindfulness meditation exercises. Thus, among empirically supported treatments, MBCT appears to provide the most comprehensive training available in the accepting, nonjudgmental, and decentered approach to internal experience that recent conceptualizations suggest may be important in the treatment of binge eating. In addition, the low proportion of change strategies in MBCT should represent a strong test of the idea that a mindfulness-based intervention can influence binge eating behavior (Kristeller, Baer, & Quillian-Wolever, 2006).

Although cognitive behavior therapy and interpersonal psychotherapy for binge eating have received more empirical support in adults with binge eating disorder than DBT (Safer et al., 2007), Corstorphine (2006) emphasized that the addition of the Mindfulness component to the cognitive behavioral therapy protocol would be a useful option, since it offers the clinician and patient an alternative when standard CBT is unsuccessful in relieving symptoms. Along the same lines, Proulx (2008) stressed that Mindfulness-based intervention would be a useful adjunct to individual or family psychotherapy for women with more severe eating disorder symptoms.

Considering all the aspects studied in the review of the papers, it would appear that mindfulness-based therapies represent promising lines of inquiry since each of the selected studies reported satisfactory results. However, more formal evaluation is needed to clarify its effectiveness and applicability (Corstorphine, 2006; Heffner et al., 2002; Baer, Fischer, & Huss, 2005).

The papers reviewed reported a very short follow-up period. It would be advisable to extend this period in future studies on the application of Mindfulness to the treatment of Eating Disorders since, as was recognized in some articles (Kristeller & Hallett, 1999; Leahey et al., 2008), there is little data to support assertions regarding long term changes due to mindfulness applications. Moreover, this has already been done in studies where mindfulness has been applied in relation to other disorders (Miller, Fletcher, & Kabat-Zinn, 1995).

## Conclusions and Future Directions

There is a small body of evidence for the efficacy of Mindfulness in Eating Disorders, but trial quality has been very variable and sample sizes have been small. Therefore, more and larger trials are needed. One option that could help to clarify the role of Mindfulness in these disorders would be to design a study that separated the formal meditation elements from those components of treatment more related to standard cognitive-behavioral therapy. Separate consideration of these factors could contribute to an understanding of the importance and effectiveness of Mindfulness in the treatment of eating disorders.

## REFERENCES

Baer, R. A., Fischer, S., & Huss, D. B. (2005). Mindfulness-based cognitive therapy applied to binge eating: a case study. *Cognitive and Behavioral Practice, 12*, 351–358.

Barrios, M., Borrego, A., Vilaginés, A., Ollé, C., & Somoza, M. (2008). A bibliometric study of psychological research on tourism. *Scientometrics, 77*, 453–467.

Corstorphine, E. (2006). Cognitive-emotional-behavioural therapy for the Eating Disorders: working with beliefs about emotions. *European Eating Disorders Review, 14*, 448–461.

Davis, L. W., Strasburger, A. M., & Brown, L. F. (2007). Mindfulness: an intervention for anxiety in schizophrenia. *Journal of Psychosocial Nursing and Mental Health Services, 45*, 23–29.

Elomaa, M. M., de C Williams, A. C., & Kalso, E. A. (2009). Attention management as a treatment for chronic pain. *European Journal of Pain, 13*, 1062–1067.

Gaylord, S. A., Whitehead, W. E., Coble, R. S., Faurot, K. R., Palsson, O. S., Garland, E. L. . . . Mann, J. D. (2009). Mindfulness for irritable bowel syndrome: Protocol development for a controlled clinical trial. *BMC Complementary and Alternative Medicine, 9*, e24.

Hart, R. L. (2007). Collaboration and article quality in the literature of academic librarianship. *The Journal of Academic Librarianship, 33*, 190–195.

Heffner, M., Sperry, J., Eifert, G. H., & Detweiler, M. (2002). Acceptance and commitment therapy in the treatment of an adolescent female with anorexia nervosa: A case example. *Cognitive and Behavioral Practice, 9*, 232–236.

Hsu, S. H., Grow, J., & Marlatt, G. A. (2008). Mindfulness and addiction. *Recent Developments in Alcoholism, 18*, 229–250.

Kristeller, J. L. & Hallett, C. B. (1999). An exploratory study of a meditation-based intervention for binge eating disorder. *Journal of Health Psychology, 4*, 357–363.

Kristeller, J. L., Baer, R. A., & Quillian-Wolever, R. (2006). Mindfulness-based approaches to eating disorders. In R. Baer R (Ed.), *Mindfulness and acceptance-based interventions: conceptualization, application, and empirical support* (pp. 75–91). San Diego, CA: Elsevier.

Lavander, J. M., Jardin, B. F., & Anderson, D. A. (2009). Bulimic symptoms in undergraduate men and women: Contributions of Mindfulness and thought suppression. *Eating Behaviors, 10*, 228–231.

Ledesma, D., & Kumano, H. (2009). Mindfulness-based stress reduction and cancer: A meta-analysis. *Psychooncology, 18*, 571–579.

Leahey, T. M., Crowther, J. H., & Irwin, S. R. (2008). A cognitive-behavioral Mindfulness group therapy intervention for the treatment of binge eating in bariatric surgery patients, *Cognitive and Behavioral Practice, 15*, 349–442.

Lush, E., Salmon, P., Floyd, A., Studts, J. L., Weissbecker, I., & Sephton S. E. (2009). Mindfulness meditation for symptom reduction in fibromyalgia: psychophysiological correlates. *Journal of Clinical Psychology in Medical Settings, 16*, 200–207.

Miller, J. J., Fletcher, K., & Kabat-Zinn, J. (1995). Three-year follow-up and clinical implications of a mindfulness meditation-based stress reduction intervention in the treatment of anxiety disorders. *General Hospital Psychiatry, 17*, 192–200.

Ong, J. C., Shapiro, S. L., & Manber, R. (2008). Combining mindfulness meditation with cognitive-behavior therapy for insomnia: A treatment-development study. *Behavior Therapy, 39*, 171–182.

Proulx, K. (2008). Experiences of women with bulimia nervosa in a mindfulness-based eating disorder treatment group. *Eating Disorders, 16*, 52–72.

Safer, D. L., Lock, J., & Couturier, J. L. (2007). Dialectical behavior therapy modified for adolescent binge eating disorder: a case report. *Cognitive and Behavioral Practice, 14*, 157–167.

Safer, D. L., Telch, C. F., & Agras, W. S. (2001). Dialectical behavior therapy adapted for bulimia: A case report. *International Journal of Eating Disorders, 30*, 101–106.

Surawy, C., Roberts, J., & Silver, A. (2005). The effect of Mindfulness training on mood and measures of fatigue, activity, and quality of life in patients with Chronic Fatigue Syndrome on a hospital waiting list: A series of exploratory studies. *Behavioural and Cognitive Psychotherapy, 33*, 103–109.

Vallejo, M. A. (2006). Mindfulness. *Papeles del Psicólogo, 27*, 92–99.

# Qualitative Chapters

# Mindfulness-Based Eating Awareness Training for Treating Binge Eating Disorder: The Conceptual Foundation

JEAN L. KRISTELLER

*Department of Psychology, Indiana State University, Terre Haute, Indiana, USA*

RUTH Q. WOLEVER

*Duke Integrative Medicine, Duke University School of Medicine, Durham, North Carolina, USA*

*This paper reviews the conceptual foundation of mindfulness-based eating awareness training (MB-EAT). It provides an overview of key therapeutic components as well as a brief review of current research. MB-EAT is a group intervention that was developed for treatment of binge eating disorder (BED) and related issues. BED is marked by emotional, behavioral and physiological disregulation in relation to food intake and self-identity. MB-EAT involves training in mindfulness meditation and guided mindfulness practices that are designed to address the core issues of BED: controlling responses to varying emotional states; making conscious food choices; developing an awareness of hunger and satiety cues; and cultivating self-acceptance. Evidence to date supports the value of MB-EAT in decreasing binge episodes, improving one's sense of self-control with regard to eating, and diminishing depressive symptoms.*

## INTRODUCTION

Mindfulness-based eating awareness training (MB-EAT; Kristeller, Baer, & Quillian-Wolever, 2006; Kristeller & Hallett, 1999; Wolever & Best, 2009) was developed specifically for treatment of binge eating disorder (BED) and related issues. BED is marked by use of food to handle emotional distress (Goldfield, Adamo, Rutherford, & Legg, 2008), along with disregulation of interoceptive awareness, appetite and satiety mechanisms (Sysko, Devlin, Walsh, Zimmerli, & Kissileff, 2007), and reactivity to food cues (Sobik, Hutchison, & Craighead, 2005). Even if familiar with nutritional recommendations for healthy eating, individuals with BED generally report frustration and a sense of inadequacy using such guidelines. Eating, food, and body weight typically play a disproportionate role as aspects of self-identity (Dunkley & Grilo, 2007). Rather than being a nurturing process, the relationship to eating and food is experienced as an internal struggle marked by intense approach and avoidance.

MB-EAT was originally informed by three theoretical approaches: models of food intake regulation that emphasize the interplay of psychological and physiological control processes (Hetherington & Rolls, 1996; Rodin, 1981), self-regulation theory (Schwartz, 1975), and neuro-cognitive and therapeutic models of mindfulness meditation (Goleman, 1988; Kristeller, 2007; Siegel, 2007). Decades of research on physiological hunger and satiety mechanisms indicate that such signals are easily overridden by non-nutritive influences (Capaldi, 1996). In particular, individuals with BED show marked imbalance and oversensitivity to "external" or "non-nutritive" cues to eat (social, emotional, or conditioned craving for certain foods), and a concomitant desensitization to "internal" cues, particularly related to normal satiety processes. While one model of this imbalance is grounded in biological (e.g., genetic or epigenetic) explanations of hedonic imbalance (Appelhans, 2009), an alternative perspective is that individuals become "disconnected" from internal experience, creating patterns of "mindless" eating (Wansink, 2007). Many binge eaters seek out traditional diet programs; these may be effective in the short term, but may further disconnect individuals from internal signals by imposing external structure with little personal flexibility or opportunity to re-learn adaptive habits, and often fail to acknowledge or address the intensity of hedonic craving.

Self-regulation theory (Schwartz, 1975; Shapiro & Schwartz, 2000) posits that internal regulatory processes in the body depend to a substantial degree on a capacity to self-observe internal states. As is the case for biofeedback, an original focus of self-regulation theory, cultivation of self-awareness of relevant internal cues can engage regulatory systems more effectively. Drawing on homeostatic models of psychobiological functioning, self-regulation theory further proposes that even complex systems can be re-regulated and maintained with relatively little sense of effort or struggle. This perspective is somewhat in contrast to self-control models that presume an ongoing need for vigilance, externally imposed structure, and effortful self-management. A primary goal of the MB-EAT program is to re-regulate the balance between physiological factors and non-nutritive factors that drive eating. Thus, by helping individuals cultivate greater awareness of hunger and satiety as well as emotional states and external triggers, MB-EAT engages self-regulatory processes related to appetite, emotional balance, and behavior.

Emerging neurocognitive models support the value of meditation practice as a path toward change (Lutz, Slagter, Dunne, & Davidson, 2008). This is particularly true for complex systems in which self-protective or appetitive drives (such as anxiety reactions or addictive processes) need to be brought into better balance through higher level neuro-processing. While meditation is recognized to have powerful impact as a "relaxation" tool, it is more appropriately viewed as a way to cultivate a particular quality of attention and awareness, which then mediates self-regulation across multiple domains of functioning, including physical, emotional, behavioral, and relationship to self and others. This multi-domain model of meditation (Kristeller, 2003, 2007) is particularly applicable to treatment of complex eating disorders since they involve disregulation in multiple domains of functioning.

The concepts of emergent "wisdom" and self-acceptance, core aspects of traditional meditation practice, also are central to the MB-EAT program. Participants are encouraged to recognize their own internal strengths, and be open to their own understanding and solutions to challenging situations, rather than reacting judgmentally to self-perceived variances from internalized norms, whether of behavior or weight, a hallmark of eating disorders. Within our framework, mindfulness meditation is conceptualized as a way of training attention to increase nonjudgmental awareness of internal experience and automatic patterns related to eating, emotional regulation, and self-acceptance. The importance of self-acceptance, compassion and forgiveness are highly relevant to interrupting the dysfunctional cycles of binging, self-recrimination, and over-restraint. Mindfulness meditation is further used to cultivate the capacity to disengage undesirable reactivity, and to engage processes that can more "wisely" inform behavior (Kristeller, 2003; Kristeller, et al., 2006; Wolever & Best, 2009). Other therapeutic applications of mindfulness meditation, such as the Mindfulness-Based Stress Reduction Program (Kabat-Zinn, 1990), Mindfulness-Based Cognitive Therapy (Segal, Williams, & Teasdale, 2002), and Mindfulness-Based Relapse Prevention (Marlatt, Bowen, & Lustyk, in press) undertake similar goals in regard to treatment of anxiety disorders, depression, and addictions, respectively. They also utilize both general training in mindfulness meditation and mindfulness exercises specific to the presenting issues and associated therapeutic needs.

The MB-EAT model is consistent with other perspectives on treating dysfunctional and highly conditioned eating patterns, including the following: the chronic dieting model (Herman & Polivy, 1980), the escape model (Heatherton & Baumeister, 1991), cognitive-behavioral approaches (Apple & Agras, 1997; Fairburn & Wilson, 1993), interpersonal therapy (Wilfley et al., 2002) for BED, and other approaches incorporating mindfulness within acceptance-based treatments (Safer, Telch, & Chen, 2009; Wilson,

2004). However, similar to Appetite Awareness Training (Allen & Craighead, 1999), MB-EAT brings more explicit attention to processes of food intake *per se*. MB-EAT also incorporates more recent work recognizing the complexity of hedonic drives associated with food (Appelhans, 2009); retraining hunger and satiety awareness may be particularly pertinent to managing such hedonic pressure in individuals particularly sensitive to this aspect of eating. In sum, the MB-EAT program is designed to help individuals cultivate awareness of both internal and external triggers to eating, interrupt dysfunctional cycles of binging, self-recrimination and over-restraint, and re-engage the natural physiological processes of eating regulation. Furthermore, the program emphasizes the pleasure and nurturing aspects of eating, while encouraging healthier patterns of food choice, in terms of both types and amount of food eaten. MB-EAT is further designed to do so in a way that is effective in internalizing and maintaining change.

## PROGRAM STRUCTURE: THE CONCEPTUAL FRAMEWORK

The MB-EAT program is structured to gradually introduce, in parallel, elements of mindfulness meditation practice, mindful eating, and themes of self-awareness and self-acceptance. Table 1 outlines key theoretical principles and concepts, treatment components reflecting each principle, and related core practices used in the 10-session treatment program.

### Cultivating Mindfulness

MB-EAT emphasizes the value of mindfulness meditation for cultivating an ability to focus attention, engage awareness, and disengage "mindless" reactivity. In addition, the program stresses the core concepts of engaging "wisdom" and the heartful qualities of mindfulness such as non-judgment, compassion, and self-acceptance. Training in mindfulness practice begins with breath awareness and sitting meditation. In Session 2, we introduce the practice of using "mini-meditations" to quiet and focus attention in the moment as a way to bring mindfulness to eating experiences. This process is later generalized to bringing mindfulness to any aspect of daily life. All sessions include mindfulness practice; participants are encouraged to practice daily at home, initially for 10 minutes, and then for 20 minutes.

### Cultivating Mindful Eating

In the first seven sessions, different mindfulness exercises are used to help individuals bring awareness to and re-balance aspects of eating that are typically disregulated in eating disorders. Each experience is introduced through a guided meditation practice, followed by discussion. Exercises target the

**TABLE 1** Components of MB-EAT: Principles and Related Exercises

| Concept/principle | Component | Session | Exercise |
|---|---|---|---|
| **1. Cultivating Mindfulness** | | | |
| a. Cultivate capacity to direct attention, be aware, disengage reactivity, and be non-judgmental. | a. Mindfulness meditation practice. | 1–10 | a. Sitting practice in session. Meditation homework. |
| b. Cultivate capacity to bring mindfulness into daily experience, including eating. | b. "Mini-meditations." General use of mindfulness. | 2–10 | b. "Mini-meditation" use. Brief practice in all sessions. |
| c. Cultivating/engaging inner and outer "wisdom." | c. Meditation practice/ mindfulness in daily life. | All sessions | c. Encouragement of insight. Wisdom meditation (Ses. 10). |
| **2. Cultivating Mindful Eating** | | | |
| a. Bring mindful attention and awareness to eating experience. Recognizing mindless eating. | a. Meditation practice. Mini-meditations. Chain reaction model. | 1–10 | a. Wide range of practices (see below for specifics). |
| b. Cultivate taste experience/ savoring and enjoying food. | b. Mindfully eating raisins. All mindful eating experiences. | 1, 2, 4, 6, 7, 9 | b. Raisins; cheese & crackers; chocolate; fruit & veggies; "favorite food"; pot luck/buffet homework. |
| c. Cultivate awareness of hunger experience. | c. Hunger awareness. | 3 | c. Hunger meditation; homework. |
| d. Awareness and cultivation of sensory-specific satiety/taste satisfaction. | d. Training in sensory specific satiety, both in and out of session. | 4, 7 | d. Taste satisfaction "meter." Pot luck/buffet homework. |
| e. Making mindful food choices, based on both "liking" and health. | e. "Inner wisdom" and "outer wisdom" in regard to food choice. Mindful decrease in calories. | 2, 4–6, 7 | e. Choice: chips, cookies, or grapes. Mindful use of nutrition info. 500 Calorie Challenge. Managing social influences. |
| f. Awareness and cultivation of fullness experience. | f. Mindfully ending a meal. | 1–6 | f. Fullness awareness/ratings. Pot luck/buffet homework. |

*(Continued)*

**TABLE 1** (*Continued*)

| Concept/principle | Component | Session | Exercise |
|---|---|---|---|
| g. Awareness of negative self-judgment regarding eating. Cultivate non-judgmental awareness of eating experience. | g. Eating challenging foods. Identifying cognitive distortions. | 2–6, 9, 10 | g. Identifying "black & white" thinking; "surfing the urge"; abstinence violation effect. |
| **3. Cultivating Emotional Balance** | | | |
| a. Cultivate awareness of emotions and emotional reactivity. | a. Learn to identify and tolerate emotional triggers. | 3–5, 9, 10 | a. Mindfulness practice; chain reaction model; mini-meditations. |
| b. Meeting emotional needs in healthy ways. | b. Behavior substitution; modifying comfort eating. | Most sessions | b. Emotional eating visualization. Savoring food. |
| **4. Cultivating Self-acceptance** | | | |
| a. Acceptance and non-selfjudgment of body/self-regulation/gentle exercise. | a. Relationship to the body. | 1, 3–5, 8 | a. Breathe awareness; body scan practice; healing self-touch; chair yoga; pedometers; mindful walking. |
| b. Recognition of anger at self and others. Acceptance of self/others. | b. Exploring feeling and thoughts toward self and others. | 4, 5, 10 | b. Loving kindness meditation. Forgiveness meditation. Discussion. |
| c. Recognizing and engaging capacity for growth. Self-empowerment. | c. Cultivating and honoring wisdom in self. | All, 10 | c. Wisdom meditation. Discussion throughout. |

following: bringing awareness to sensations of physical hunger and different types of satiety (stomach fullness and sensory-specific satiety); bringing mindfulness to eating all types/categories of food with a focus on gaining hedonic pleasure from small quantities of food; awareness of non-nutritive triggers for eating and making particular food choices. The first guided experience is borrowed from MBSR: mindfully eating three raisins. Emphasis is placed on noticing and amplifying each sensation, noting thoughts and feelings while eating the raisin, observing flavor and texture preferences, and savoring each raisin as fully as possible. Participants generally share amazement at the intensity of the experience, the distinctness of each raisin, and awareness of how the experience differs from "mindlessly" eating a handful of raisins all at once.

Six sessions have an embedded mindful eating practice. After the first mindful eating experience with raisins, the foods are increasingly challenging in terms of hedonic and caloric value. Common snack foods with lower nutritional value are used to bring mindful awareness to potential "binge" foods. This also engages the "liking" vs. "wanting" distinction, of increasing interest in the experimental food regulation literature (Finlayson, King, & Blundell, 2007). In Session 2, participants eat cheese and crackers mindfully, and in Session 4, chocolate brownies. In Session 5, they mindfully choose to eat two of three possible snack foods: corn chips, a butter cookie, or grapes. This exercise increases awareness of how they make food choices, encourages consideration of healthier vs. less healthy food choices, and cultivates awareness of "taste satisfaction," our term for "sensory specific satiety." Once individuals become more attuned to the sensory experience, they often express surprise at how their chosen "snack" is less appealing (saltier or greasier or less flavorful) than anticipated, with pleasure quickly peaking and then fading rapidly. Session 7 includes a pot-luck meal, to which participants bring two dishes: one that reflects a "healthier" style of eating; and one that is a favorite food difficult to eat in moderation (e.g., macaroni and cheese). The meal is begun in silence and offers guidelines around mindfully returning for "seconds," encouragement to leave food on the plate, and reminders to choose "quality over quantity."

Session 3 introduces the exploration of the experience of physical hunger, as distinct from emotional hunger. Participants are asked to note how physically hungry they are on a 10-point scale, with 10 being *as hungry as possible*, and 1 being *not hungry at all*. They are then asked to clarify the physical signals used to determine hunger ratings. In session 4, awareness of fullness is introduced by having participants drink a large bottle of water, also using a 10-point scale, to rate fullness. Using a second scale makes clear that hunger and fullness are not just opposite ends of a scale but overlap, because they are controlled by distinct, although related, mechanisms. Use of water also emphasizes that stomach distention is somewhat separate from caloric intake, underscoring the complexity of these processes.

Homework related to mindful eating begins with the challenge to eat one meal or snack mindfully each day, increasing to eating all meals and snacks mindfully. Initial assignments focus on single aspects of mindful eating (e.g., flavor, pace, attention to hunger) to build specific skills. Later assignments encourage integration of multiple skills by simultaneously attending to physical hunger, food choice, flavor, texture, fullness, thoughts, and feelings before and throughout eating. For example, after the pot luck meal, the homework includes going to an "all you can eat" buffet. The assignment entails use of all of the eating practices to date under inherently difficult circumstances, an important learning experience, given the frequent challenges of family meals or parties.

## Cultivating Emotional Balance

There is no question that eating meets emotional needs, more for some individuals than others. Mindfulness practice is used to help cultivate awareness of emotional triggers and eating patterns, as a way to interrupt the chain of reactivity, and a way to contribute to emotional well-being. A chain reaction exercise, adapted from Dialectical Behavior Therapy for eating disorders (Wisniewski & Kelly, 2003), helps capture the complexity of over-conditioned responses, accompanied by the message that the links in the chain can be uncoupled at many points, even in the midst of a binge. The link between harsh self-judgment, over-eating, and negative affect is addressed, along with common types of distorted thinking that usually serve to further the cycle of disordered eating and negative mood. One common thought distortion is the abstinence violation effect ("I've blown it, so I might as well keep going;" Marlatt & Gordon, 1985). Work with such cognitive distortions is expanded from eating behavior to a wider range of experience. Participants are also encouraged to explore alternatives to eating as ways to meet their emotional needs; at the same time, they are encouraged to savor their own preferred "comfort" foods in smaller quantities, with a focus on quality.

## Cultivating Self-Acceptance

Another theme of the program is developing a better relationship with the self, including the physical self, self-identity, and self in relation to others. A body scan exercise encourages distinguishing between experiencing the body and judging the body. This is followed by gentle chair yoga in Session 5, and mindful walking in Session 8, which serve to further increase awareness of the body while simultaneously cultivating an attitude of kindness and compassion. Chair yoga is used instead of floor yoga because individuals whose BMI is over 40 (the average weight of our treatment participants) may have significant difficulty getting down to the floor. Furthermore, chair yoga encourages use of gentle yoga stretches within usual daily routines (such as at a desk or table). Mindful walking, at varying speeds, helps bring a quality of awareness into daily activity as well as to the process of moving the body, to appreciation for what the body can do, and to recognition of its needs. Finally, a healing self-touch exercise[1] often has profound impact, as participants are directed to fill their hands with loving kindness, and place them onto various parts of their bodies. They begin with areas they like and appreciate, and move on to extend appreciation to areas with which they struggle.

The theme of self-acceptance is extended beyond the body to shifting one's relationship to other aspects of the self. Participants are consistently encouraged to engage an attitude of curiosity and non-judgmental exploration of thoughts, feelings, and bodily states. Self-care is reinforced throughout, including active enjoyment and taking pleasure in eating. The delicate balance between accountability and self-blame is explored in a guided Forgiveness Meditation in Session 5. The meditation explores release of anger both at oneself and at others while also encouraging learning from these observations. It is not unusual that individuals recognize how such anger is driving their patterns of binging and self-recrimination. Self-acceptance and confidence regarding interpersonal interactions are explored throughout the program in the context of negotiating social pressures to eat from friends or family members. Self-acceptance is buoyed throughout the entire program as individuals are encouraged to recognize their own "inner wisdom" and cultivate it through meditation. This "inner wisdom" framework is referred to from the first session through the end, culminating as the primary theme of Session 10 with a guided Wisdom Meditation. The emphasis is on recognizing one's own inner wisdom and using it to create a path to wise choice, informed by general knowledge, but guided by experience and internal resources.

## EMPIRICAL SUPPORT FOR MB-EAT

The original proof of concept study used a non-randomized, extended baseline/follow-up design (Kristeller & Hallett, 1999), with a completed sample of 18 obese women (out of 20 enrolled) who met criteria for BED (avg. age = 46.5; mean weight = 238 lbs.; mean BMI: 40). They participated in a 7-session group program over 6 weeks. Binges per week dropped from over 4 to about 1.5. By self-report, amount of food consumed during remaining binges decreased substantially, although four participants still met criteria for BED at 1 month follow-up. Scores on the Binge Eating Scale (BES; Gormally, Black, Daston, & Rardin, 1982) fell from the "severe" range to just higher

---

[1]    The healing self-touch exercise was developed by Sasha Loring, MS, MEd at Duke Integrative Medicine.

than having "little or no problem" with binge eating. Depression decreased from clinical to sub-clinical levels. The strongest predictor of improvement in eating control was time spent using eating related meditations.

Subsequently, an NIH-funded two-site randomized clinical trial (Kristeller, Wolever & Sheets, under review) randomized participants with similar characteristics (total $N = 140$; 15% men) to three arms: MB-EAT; a psycho-educational (PE) treatment based on the Duke Diet and Fitness Center obesity treatment program; or a waiting list, with follow-up at 1 and 4 months. The treatment expanded to 9 sessions and included greater emphasis on body experience and the heartful qualities of mindfulness: non-judgment, compassion, and cultivation of self-acceptance. As has been reported in other studies comparing new interventions to other active interventions, the MB-EAT and PE groups showed somewhat similar improvements in behavior and on the BES. However, improvement in the MB-EAT group was greater or approached significance on measures indicative of internalizing change (e.g., the Hunger scale of the Three Factor Eating Questionnaire; Stunkard & Messick, 1985). Depression also improved in both groups but appeared to be for different reasons. The improvement in the PE group was linked to decreased bingeing, while the improvement in MB-EAT was linked to amount of meditation practice. Amount of meditation practice also predicted improvement on other indicators of self-regulation, including lost weight. Use of eating-related meditations and "mini-meditations" accounted for more of the variance than did general sitting meditation.

A recently completed trial (Kristeller, 2010) broadened recruitment to include those with a BMI of at least 35; 25% met criteria for clinical or subclinical (one binge/week) BED. The treatment expanded to 10 sessions (as outlined in Table 1), with two follow-up sessions, and includes additional components addressing "outer wisdom" specific to caloric and nutritional guidelines. These components explore how to use such guidelines in a personally sustainable way to encourage individuals to move toward weight loss, in addition to rebalancing eating patterns. The "inner wisdom" themes of hunger, satiety, and choice awareness remain the same, with exercises to encourage re-regulation of eating behaviors without a sense of struggle or self-recrimination. Preliminary analyses indicate that participants with BED showed comparable improvement to those without BED, including a weight loss of about 7 lbs. at immediate post, with equivalent retention in the study. Improvement on other key variables appears comparable to that observed in our previous research.

## CONCLUSION

The MB-EAT program combines well understood principles of food intake regulation and principles of mindfulness meditation to provide a novel approach to re-regulating eating behavior. While conceptually compatible with other effective approaches to treating eating disorders, it is unique in several respects. First, training in mindfulness meditation serves as a foundation for cultivating a capacity to bring non-judgmental awareness to the complex processes involved in food choice, the decision to initiate eating, and the decision to stop eating. Second, the training helps people systematically re-engage innate abilities to use hunger and satiety signals. Third, the training purposefully cultivates drawing pleasure from eating, by emphasizing "quality over quantity" in doing so. Finally, MB-EAT encourages an attitude of non-judgmental acceptance of self to daily living, body awareness and emotional experiences, beginning with food-related experiences and expanding to the whole self.

Research has demonstrated the effectiveness of MB-EAT in treating compulsive eating patterns associated with binge eating disorder. Ongoing research further suggests that MB-EAT can be adapted to address weight loss, without losing its effectiveness for treating the associated symptoms of binge eating. Further work is needed to explore its application to normalizing relationship to food and eating for both the compulsive and restrictive aspects of food intake associated with bulimia nervosa and anorexia nervosa.

# REFERENCES

Allen, H., & Craighead, L. (1999). Appetite monitoring in the treatment of binge eating disorder. *Behavior Therapy, 30*, 253–272.

Appelhans, B. M. (2009). Neurobehavioral inhibition of reward-driven feeding: Implications for dieting and obesity. *Obesity, 17*, 640–647.

Apple, R. A., & Agras, W. S. (1997). *Overcoming eating disorders: A cognitive-behavioral treatment for bulimia and binge-eating disorder*. New York, NY: Psychological Corporation.

Capaldi, E. D. (Ed.). (1996). *Why we eat what we eat: The psychology of eating*. Washington, DC: American Psychological Association.

Dunkley, D. M., & Grilo, C. M. (2007). Self-criticism, low self-esteem, depressive symptoms, and over-evaluation of shape and weight in binge eating disorder patients. *Behaviour Research & Therapy, 45*, 139–149.

Fairburn, C. G., & Wilson, G. T. (1993). *Binge eating: Nature, assessment, and treatment*. New York, NY: Guilford Press.

Finlayson, G., King, N., & Blundell, J. E. (2007). Liking vs. wanting food: Importance for human appetite control and weight regulation. *Neuroscience and Biobehavioral Reviews, 31*, 987–1002.

Goldfield, G. S., Adamo, K. B., Rutherford, J., & Legg, C. (2008). Stress and the relative reinforcing value of food in female binge eaters. *Physiology & Behavior, 93*, 579–587.

Goleman, D. (1988). *The meditative mind: The varieties of meditative experience*. New York, NY: G. P. Putnam & Sons.

Gormally, J., Black, S., Daston, S., & Rardin, D. (1982). The assessment of binge eating severity among obese persons. *Addictive Behaviors, 7*(1), 47–55.

Heatherton, T. F., & Baumeister, R. F. (1991). Binge eating as escape from self-awareness. *Psychological Bulletin, 110,* 86–108.

Herman, C., & Polivy, J. (1980). Restrained eating. In A. Stunkard (Ed.), *Obesity* (pp. 208–225). Philadelphia, PA: Saunders.

Hetherington, M. M., & Rolls, B. J. (1996). Sensory-specific satiety: Theoretical frameworks and central characteristics. In E. D. Capaldi (Ed.), *Why we eat what we eat: The psychology of eating.* (pp. 267–290). Washington, DC: American Psychological Association.

Kabat-Zinn, J. (1990). *Full catastrophe living.* New York. NY: Delacorte Press.

Kristeller, J. L. (2003). Mindfulness, wisdom and eating: Applying a multi-domain model of meditation effects. *Journal of Constructivism in the Human Sciences, 8,* 107–118.

Kristeller, J. L. (2007). Mindfulness meditation. In P. Lehrer, R. Wookfolk & W. E. Simes (Eds.), *Principles and practices of stress management* (3rd ed., pp. 393–427). New York, NY: Guilford Press.

Kristeller, J. L. (2010, April). *Mindfulness-based eating awareness training (MB-EAT): Theory, research, and practice.* Paper presented at the Society of Behavioral Medicine, Seattle, WA.

Kristeller, J. L., Baer, R. A., & Quillian-Wolever, R. (2006). Mindfulness-based approaches to eating disorders. In R. A. Baer (Ed.), *Mindfulness-based treatment approaches* (pp. 75–91). Burlington, MA: Academic Press.

Kristeller, J. L., & Hallett, C. B. (1999). An exploratory study of a meditation-based intervention for binge eating disorder. *Journal of Health Psychology, 4,* 357–363.

Lutz, A., Slagter, H. A., Dunne, J. D., & Davidson, R. J. (2008). Attention regulation and monitoring in meditation. *Trends in Cognitive Sciences, 12*(4), 163–169.

Marlatt, G. A., Bowen, S. W., & Lustyk, K. (in press). Substance abuse and relapse prevention. In C. K. Germer & R. D. Siegel (Eds.), *Compassion and wisdom in psychotherapy.* New York, NY: Guilford Press.

Marlatt, G. A., & Gordon, J. R. (Eds.). (1985). *Relapse prevention: Maintenance strategies in the treatment of addictive behaviors.* New York, NY: Guilford Press.

Rodin, J. (1981). Current status of the internal-external hypothesis for obesity: What went wrong? *American Psychologist, 36,* 361–372.

Safer, D. L., Telch, C. F., & Chen, E. Y. (2009). *Dialectical behavior therapy for binge eating and bulimia.* New York, NY: Guilford Press.

Schwartz, G. E. (1975). Biofeedback, self-regulation, and the patterning of physiological processes. *American Scientist, 63,* 314–324.

Segal, Z. V., Williams, J. M. G., & Teasdale, J. D. (2002). *Mindfulness-based cognitive therapy for depression: A new approach to preventing relapse.* New York, NY: Guilford Press.

Shapiro, S. L., & Schwartz, G. E. (2000). The role of intention in self-regulation: Toward intentional systemic mindfulness. In M. Boekaerts, P. R. Pintrich & M. Zeidner (Eds.), *Handbook of self-regulation* (pp. 253–273). San Diego, CA: Academic Press.

Siegel, D. J. (2007). *The mindful brain.* New York, NY: W. W. Norton.

Sobik, L., Hutchison, K., & Craighead, L. (2005). Cue-elicited craving for food: A fresh approach to the study of binge eating. *Appetite, 44,* 253–261.

Stunkard, A. J., & Messick, S. (1985). The Three Factor Eating Questionnaire to measure dietary restraint, disinhibition and hunger. *Journal of Psychosomatic Research, 29*(1), 71–83.

Sysko, R., Devlin, M. J., Walsh, B. T., Zimmerli, E., & Kissileff, H. R. (2007). Satiety and test meal intake among women with binge eating disorder. *International Journal of Eating Disorders, 40,* 554–561.

Wansink, B. (2007). *Mindless eating: Why we eat more than we think.* New York, NY: Bantam Books.

Wilfley, D. E., Welch, R. R., Stein, R. I., Spurrell, E. B., Cohen, L. R., Saelens, B. E. . . . Matt, G.E.. (2002). A randomized comparison of group cognitive-behavioral therapy and group interpersonal psychotherapy for the treatment of overweight individuals with binge-eating disorder. *Archives of General Psychiatry, 59,* 713–721.

Wilson, G. T. (2004). Acceptance and change in the treatment of eating disorders: The evolution of manual-based cognitive-behavioral therapy. In S. C. Hayes, V. M. Follette & M. M. Linehan (Eds.), *Mindfulness and acceptance: Expanding the cognitive-behavioral tradition.* (pp. 243–260). New York, NY: Guilford Press.

Wisniewski, L., & Kelly, E. (2003). The application of dialectical behavior therapy to the treatment of eating disorders. *Cognitive and Behavioral Practice, 10,* 131–138.

Wolever, R. Q., & Best, J. L. (2009). Mindfulness-based approaches to eating disorders. In F. Didonna (Ed.), *Clinical handbook of mindfulness* (pp. 259–288). New York, NY: Springer.

# Psychological Inflexibility and Symptom Expression in Anorexia Nervosa

RHONDA M. MERWIN

*Department of Psychiatry and Behavioral Sciences, Duke University Medical Center,*
*Durham, North Carolina, USA*

C. ALIX TIMKO

*Department of Behavioral and Social Sciences, University of the Sciences, Philadelphia,*
*Pennsylvania, USA*

ASHLEY A. MOSKOVICH

*Department of Psychology and Neuroscience, Duke University,*
*Durham, North Carolina, USA*

KRISTA KONRAD INGLE

*Department of Psychology, Meredith College, Raleigh, North Carolina, USA*

CYNTHIA M. BULIK

*Department of Psychiatry, University of North Carolina-Chapel Hill,*
*Chapel Hill, North Carolina, USA*

NANCY L. ZUCKER

*Department of Psychiatry and Behavioral Sciences, Duke University Medical Center; and*
*Department of Psychology and Neuroscience, Duke University,*
*Durham, North Carolina, USA*

*The purpose of this article is to outline a model of anorexia nervosa (AN) as a disorder of psychological inflexibility, motivated by an insatiable desire for prediction and control with related intolerance for uncertainty. We describe preliminary data that provide initial support for this conceptualization and point to the ways in which mindfulness and acceptance-based strategies might be particularly useful for treating AN. This article is not intended to be*

This work is supported by National Institute of Mental Health (NIMH) grants K23-MH-070418 (Principal investigator: Zucker), R01-MH-07821 (Principal investigator: Zucker) and RC1-MH-088678 (Principal investigator: Zucker.)

*an exhaustive literature review, rather a conceptual framework to guide future research and treatment development.*

# INTRODUCTION

*An emaciated 15-year-old painstakingly and meticulously places dry cereal into a measuring cup, leveling it 3 times with a knife and carefully checking the box to ensure the caloric information has not changed since she read the box this morning. Unaware of her hunger, the helpless stare from her father, or the amount of time that has passed, she focuses only on whether the piece of cereal rupturing the smooth surface should be removed or perhaps the piece next to it as well. . . .*

Anorexia nervosa (AN) is a devastating illness in which behavior is profoundly narrow, rigid, and seemingly disconnected from somatic experience. This behavioral profile, when combined with the self-imposed starvation pathognomonic of the disorder, contributes to the designation of eating disorders as one of the 10 leading causes of disability among women (Mathers, Vos, Stevenson, & Begg, 2000; Striegel-Moore & Bulik, 2007). While advances have been made in the management of adolescent AN (Keel & Haedt, 2008; Lock & Fitzpatrick, 2009); a significant minority fail to directly benefit from treatment (Eisler, Simic, Russell, & Dare, 2007), comorbid psychopathology persists (Herpertz-Dahlmann et al., 2001), and crossover to other forms of eating disorders is common (Eddy et al., 2008; Tozzi et al., 2005). Moreover, recommended treatments for adults with AN remain elusive (Berkman, Lohr, & Bulik, 2007; Bulik, Berkman, Brownley, Sedway, & Lohr, 2007; Wilson, Grilo, & Vitousek, 2007).

Numerous elegant models inform the pathophysiology and phenomenology of AN (Kaye, Fudge, & Paulus, 2009; Schmidt & Treasure, 2006; Steinglass & Walsh, 2006). This article aims to augment existing models of AN by providing a framework from which to understand the seemingly relentless fight against the body that is characteristic of the disorder. We begin by proposing a model of AN as an illness of psychological inflexibility, defined as an inability to behave flexibly in the presence of difficult thoughts, feelings, and bodily sensations. We propose that among individuals with AN, fear of harm and demand for certainty lead to over-reliance on verbally ascribed rules for behavior to minimize ambiguity, avoid mistakes, and provide the semblance of control over aspects of experience that are essentially uncontrollable (i.e., the volatility of the body associated with motivational states such as hunger or affect). We further propose that this inflexibility motivates symptom expression. We describe how rules for behavior provide an illusion of safety and certainty, thereby allowing for short-term relief, but at the expense of long-term physical and psychological health which require sensitivity to fluctuations in experience to respond to dynamic emotional and metabolic needs. Subsequently, we review emerging research that supports the clinical relevance of psychological inflexibility for the prognosis and differentiation of AN (e.g., psychological flexibility changing in tandem with symptom remission) and explore ways in which mindfulness might facilitate flexible interaction with difficult thoughts and feelings and expand behavioral options in the presence of heightened arousal or states of uncertainty. In conclusion, we comment on areas for future research and treatment development.

## ANOREXIA NERVOSA: A MODEL OF PSYCHOLOGICAL INFLEXIBILITY

### Challenge of Controlling the Experience of the Body

Individuals with AN behave as if they are at war with their bodies, fighting for dominance or complete control. Inevitably, this is a losing battle. There are far too many fluctuating variables determining the condition of the body at any given moment for somatic states to be precisely manipulated (or "controlled"). For example, consider the factors that maintain energy homeostasis. While the energy demands of the body on any given day can be approximated with various equations (Harris & Benedict, 1919), in fact, these demands constantly vary. Such energy needs are a result of "controllable factors" such as diet and exercise combined with innumerable, "uncontrollable" internal factors that, while contributing to metabolic demands, are inaccessible to conscious manipulation (e.g., degree of muscle repair and growth, energy cost of digestion, etc). Augmenting this array of controllable and uncontrollable factors are other dynamic variables such as stage of development, status of menstrual cycle, stress, and sleep, among other variables. As if this were not complex enough, the metabolic demands of the body are recursive not linear—when we fight against the body by denying basic needs, the body "fights back" via metabolic adaptations.

Emotion is another example of a multi-systemic body experience that, like energy storage and use, eludes complete and absolute control. Consider the automaticity of sympathetic and parasympathetic (Bradley & Lang, 2007) nervous system activity in the presence of an unpleasant stimulus (e.g., a threatening gesture), or a previously benign stimulus that has acquired aversive qualities due to past experiences. Direct attempts to suppress the arousal that accompanies activation often have paradoxical effects, serving only to intensify the emotional experience (Gross & Levenson, 1997). Further, spontaneous recovery occurs, such that if arousal is deconditioned (i.e., an object that caused fear ceases to cause fear), a fear reaction may resurface without warning (Bouton, 1994; Wilson & Hayes, 1996). Repeatedly, data on suppression of panic, pain, and trauma, to name a few, demonstrate that despite our best efforts, the internal world cannot be manipulated or controlled to the same degree as some aspects of the world outside the skin (Hayes, Wilson, Gifford, Follette, & Strosahl, 1996; Merwin, Rosenthal, & Coffey, 2009).

For most individuals, fluctuations in need and bodily experience are par for the course. For example, in times of increased hunger, many people simply eat more to meet this demand. However, for individuals with AN, anxious temperament and accompanying demand for certainty (Godart et al., 2003; Godart, Flament, Perdereau, & Jeammet, 2002; Halmi et al., 2000; Lilenfeld, Wonderlich, Riso, Crosby, & Mitchell, 2006; Raney et al., 2008; Strober, Freeman, Lampert, & Diamond, 2007) may make this somatic variability intolerable and propel desperate attempts to force homeostasis. Individuals with AN may use extreme behaviors such as fasting and excessive exercise to control biological needs and stifle related motivational drives. Because the complexity of the body precludes precise prediction and control, imperfect solutions may contribute to the experience of the body as confusing, feared, or otherwise undesirable. The result may be increasingly stringent and extreme attempts to manipulate experience. Distress from even minor perturbations in somatic experience may contribute to well-established behavioral features in AN, such as perpetual error monitoring (e.g., body checking, weighing). These attempts to reduce feelings of fear and uncertainty are a logical, though maladaptive, response when one is trying to control such a naturally volatile system. Thus, those with AN may attempt to further manipulate those variables over which they have control (diet and exercise), redirecting attention away from aspects of experience that are more amorphous and less amendable to direct change. The result is an extreme state of biological and emotional suppression, a state highly reinforcing for those who demand certainty. Although this is theoretical, early descriptions of AN (e.g., Bruch, 1973) and the narratives of individuals with the illness support this notion (Serpell, Treasure, Teasdale, & Sullivan, 1999). There is also growing empirical evidence for the relationship between AN symptomatology and fear or nonacceptance of emotional responses (Merwin, Moskovich, & Zucker, 2010; Merwin, Zucker, Lacy, & Elliott, 2010; Wildes, Ringham, & Marcus, 2010).

## Verbally Ascribed Rules are the Solution (and the Problem)

The manner in which the symptoms of AN provide a sense of predictability, safety, and control (Schmidt & Treasure, 2006; Serpell et al., 1999) has occupied philosophers, clinicians, and researchers since AN was first recognized as a disorder of the mind (Brumberg, 1985, 1988). We maintain that AN does so because it provides clear rules for behavior, bypassing and attenuating volatile somatic-affective experiences which are less certain and have greater likelihood of error. Indeed, verbal rules decrease ambiguity and provide a precise road map to guide complex decisions. In the context of AN, rules dictate when and what to eat, and how much, among other decisions. Not only does this make attending to internal experience less important, but also the verbal rules themselves and associated reliance on cognitive channels may actually dampen somatic sensations. Dampening is particularly likely if those rules result in significant weight loss which perpetuates physiological adaptations that attenuate arousal. Indeed, with prolonged starvation, there is robust evidence of increased parasympathetic influence (Miller, Redlich, & Steiner, 2003), and bradycardia is a well-known adaptation to inadequate nutritional stores (Mitchell & Crow, 2006). Such physiological adaptation would be expected to reduce the overall intensity of affect (Craig, 2004), and, along with the muting of hunger cues that occurs after pronounced neglect (Wang, Hung, & Randall, 2006), promote feelings of behavioral control. In this way, individuals with AN have found an internal control strategy that does indeed "work" because it directly impacts physiological functioning, and thus effectively reduces aversive somatic-affective experience. However, while negatively reinforcing, overreliance on verbal rules for behavior also has costs.

Laboratory-based studies have demonstrated that verbal rules can interfere with learning from experience (Hayes, Thompson, & Hayes, 1989; Hayes, Brownstein, Haas, & Greenway, 1986; Hayes, Brownstein, Zettle, & Rosenfarb, 1986; Wulfert, Greenway, Farkas, & Hayes, 1994). This research has shown that when individuals are given verbal instructions about how to perform a task (e.g., "press the button fast to earn points" in a computer game) they are likely to follow that rule even when conditions change and the strategy is no longer effective in achieving reward (e.g., pushing the button slowly earns more points). This is in contrast to when individuals are in this same situation without verbal instruction. Without direct instruction, individuals will adopt a strategy based on their experience of what works (e.g., to win points) and more readily change this strategy when the conditions change. Thus, although verbal rules are extremely useful, reducing the need for prolonged trial-and-error learning, they can also interfere with the ability to learn directly from experience that may shape more adaptive behavior or otherwise maximize outcome. This has been called *rule-based insensitivity*, and refers to the phenomenon that under some conditions, individuals fail to adjust behavior to match the conditions of the environment due to competing verbal rules. Of importance, rule-based insensitivity is potentiated among those who score high on a measure of self-reported rigidity (Wulfert et al., 1994), a characteristic common among individuals with AN and likely exacerbated in the acute ill state. Thus, the more premorbid rigidity among individuals with AN, the greater the reliance on rules rather than experience, and the more starved they get, the more rigidly rule-governed they become.

In the ideal scenario, verbal instructions are flexibly integrated with direct experience. For example, while we have guidelines about when and how much to eat; our behavior is also determined by our past experience of eating to alleviate the physical discomfort of hunger. Thus, we might notice that it is 6:00 pm (a verbal guideline about meal time) and then check in with our hunger to determine whether to eat and how much. In the case of AN, verbal guidelines about eating, exercise, and the like, are applied rigidly to the neglect of direct experience. Not only does this result in a failure to meet basic needs (e.g., energy deficits resulting from pre-determined calorie limits), but it also prohibits corrective experiences. In this way, the solution is the problem; adopting rules for behavior decreases anxiety associated with ambiguity, but it also disrupts reinforcement learning that would allow individuals with AN to use somatic-affective cues more effectively.

Neuroimaging studies of adults with AN who have been weight-restored and free of eating disorder symptoms for a significant duration of time provide partial evidence for the applicability of this to individuals with AN. In a study by Wagner and colleagues (2007), individuals with AN demonstrated decreased activation in neural regions implicated in reinforcement learning. Further, whereas control subjects demonstrated variability in patterns of activation depending on the momentary results of their choice, those with AN did not evidence such variability and thus were less responsive to momentary feedback on their choices in a learning task. Further, among AN participants, neural regions associated with coding the outcomes of effort and supervisory control were more active (Wagner et al., 2007). This study, as well as others (Steinglass, Walsh, & Stern, 2006; Tchanturia et al., 2004) provide corroborating evidence that among individuals with AN, a narrow focus on rules expected to generate particular outcomes might interfere with the ability respond effectively to changing contingencies of the moment.

## Minimizing Threat: Using Verbal Rules in Social Situations

There are two potential ways to dampen uncomfortable arousal. One way is to attempt to directly manipulate the state of the body (e.g., using verbal rules about diet and exercise), another way is to reduce contact with sources of perceived threat. AN principally emerges in adolescence, when the threat of social rejection by peers is paramount (Forbes & Dahl, 2010; Hudson, Hiripi, Pope, & Kessler, 2007). In adolescents and adults with AN, research has repeatedly illustrated heightened interpersonal sensitivity and fears of negative evaluation (Broberg, Hjalmers, & Nevonen, 2001; Herpertz-Dahlmann et al., 2001; Kaye, Bulik, Thornton, Barbarich, & Masters, 2004). Reducing the threat of social rejection (and thus the accompanying anxious arousal) may be accomplished via a number of strategies. For example, using restriction to achieve a thin-ideal might function in part, to reduce threat and increase comfort in social situations by conforming to societal standards of attractiveness and the like. However, individuals with AN might also do other things to reduce risk. For example, they may directly avoid evocative social situations (e.g., not participating in less structured social activities, not self-disclosing personal information). And, of prime relevance to the current paper, they might also use the strategy that they have found useful in other domains i.e., following rules for behavior that reduce ambiguity and provide a sense of control.

Rules regarding how to behave in social situations or "social scripts" can be quite useful, providing guidelines on how to behave in novel situations, managing impressions, and allowing individuals to gain acceptance. For individuals with AN, such a strategy may be employed rigidly to reduce perceived risk of rejection and provide an organizing frame to manage complex social interactions (Zucker et al., 2007). This strategy would likely be "effective" in attenuating immediate social anxiety. However, in much the same way that individuals with AN body check or weigh to establish the accuracy of their solutions, they might also be compelled to scan or monitor the social environment for signs of error (particularly given the ultimate lack of control one has over the opinion of others). This tendency would be expected to lead to increased attention to social threat cues, such as rejecting facial expressions from others. Monitoring for social error is actually quite adaptive in order to adjust one's behavior to the demands of the situation. However, it becomes problematic when it limits the scope of information available or generates other forms of cognitive or behavioral rigidity.

Increased attention to social error and the narrowing of behavioral options to those that facilitate self-preservation may worsen or perpetuate social dysfunction among individuals with AN. In those with AN, displaying a behavioral repertoire overwhelmed by the motivation to protect against threat and mask vulnerability may contribute to perception of individuals with AN as cold, stilted, or aloof. Moreover, this pattern of visually guided attention may limit the scope of stimuli available to guide behavior and lead to a failure to perceive social nuances and positive cues. Thus, the very sensitivity to rejection which aims for self-preservation may inadvertently increase the likelihood of social failure and thus increase anxiety. Greater anxious arousal would be expected to generate increased attention *toward* the body and *away from* social stimuli. As a result of these processes, individuals with AN may cling ever more tightly to rigid rules as a solution to the overwhelming complexity of interpersonal interactions and fail to notice and implement alternative behaviors that would be more effective.

Thus, we are postulating two sources of interference with optimal learning in social situations: biased attention that decreases the range of information available to update verbal rules, and a failure to adapt verbal rules and use them flexibly based on new information. We propose that unlike the realm of diet and exercise in which rigid rules ultimately leads to reductions in aversive arousal, over time, using social scripts may actually create circumstances that facilitate *more frequent or intense* negative affect. The end result is an interpersonal system that is largely ineffective (Zucker et al., 2007) and a further retreat to the world of the body and AN, which promises to bring acceptance and at least provides a direct target for change. Although the reasons are complex and likely interact to potentiate dysfunction, this is consistent with data that indicate poorer interpersonal functioning and greater interpersonal distrust is associated with poorer prognosis and a more chronic illness course (Goodwin & Fitzgibbon, 2002; Wentz, Gillberg, Anckarsater, Gillberg, & Rastam, 2009).

Thus far, we have described how the symptoms of AN can be understood as attempts to minimize the risk of somatic-affective volatility by over-reliance on verbal rules for behavior and by monitoring for errors. Although these behavioral strategies increase the experience of prediction and control, they also directly interfere with building a meaningful, rich life—both in harmony with the body and in sync with other people (See Figure 1). Such a behavioral system exemplifies *psychological inflexibility,* a focus of recent advances in behavior therapy which emphasize the way in which diverse symptom presentations may function to regulate affect or control other aspects of internal experience (Barlow, Allen, & Choate, 2004; Hayes et al., 1996). Such therapies are further distinguished by the use of acceptance and mindfulness strategies and philosophies to increase behavioral options. Some of these newer approaches (e.g., Acceptance and Commitment Therapy; ACT) specifically integrate the role of language and cognition in promoting and maintaining maladaptive rigidity, such as that imposed by verbal rules. In the next section, we describe data that support the utility of targeting psychological inflexibility in treatment of AN. First we briefly review data that indicate effectiveness of these newer behavior

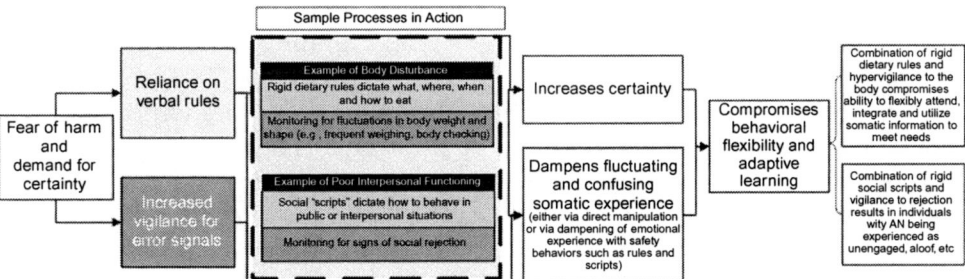

**FIGURE 1** Hypothesized systems of control in AN. Viewing the diagram from left to right, we illustrate how systems of control are both negatively and positively reinforced in two domains that are relevant for those with AN: the experience of their bodies and their relationships with others.

therapies which are increasingly being used to treat eating disorders. We then point to emerging research that suggests an improved capacity to accept and act in the presence of difficult thoughts and feelings occurs in tandem with AN symptom improvement.

## PSYCHOLOGICAL INFLEXIBILITY AS A THERAPEUTIC TARGET

### Data Supporting the Use of Acceptance and Mindfulness-Based Treatments With AN

According to our conceptualization of AN, treatment should aim to help individuals with AN to tolerate uncertainty, risk negative outcomes, and behave in new ways that are unscripted but guided by momentary feedback. To this end, strategies which shift effort away from avoidance and control and toward observing and welcoming present-moment thoughts and feelings may be particularly useful. Such strategies would not only be expected to generate increased variability in behavior so that responses may be shaped more adaptively by ongoing experiences, but also may decrease the need for eating disorder symptoms that facilitate avoidance. The end result may be development or refinement of a crucial regulatory capacity, and more efficient reinforcement learning. Specifically, observing internal experience would be expected to improve the ability to discriminate and use somatic-affective cues to guide behavior. Further, because these strategies increase openness to all internal and external events, individuals with AN would be expected to improve in their capacity to learn from ongoing feedback. Ultimately, they would be more able to use verbal rules as guides that are amendable to the unique demands of the situation and broader life goals. Facilitating effective action in the presence of heightened emotional arousal, depressogenic thoughts, and the like, is the stated goal of acceptance and mindfulness strategies which form the backbone of Acceptance and Commitment Therapy (ACT), Mindfulness-Based Cognitive Therapy (MBCT), and Dialectical Behavioral Therapy (DBT), among others.

Preliminary data on the use of acceptance and mindfulness-based treatments for eating disorders have demonstrated improvements in eating disorder symptoms, quality of life, and related psychopathology including anxiety and depression across eating disorder diagnostic categories (Baer, Fischer, & Huss, 2005a, 2005b; Berman, Boutelle, & Crow, 2009; Heffner, Sperry, Eifert, & Detweiler, 2002; Kristeller & Hallett, 1999; Safer, Lock, & Couturier, 2007; Safer, Telch, & Agras, 2001a, 2001b; Salbach-Andrae, Bohnekamp, Pfeiffer, Lehmkuhl, & Miller, 2008; Telch, Agras, & Linehan, 2000, 2001). Overall, these treatments are well tolerated and have relatively low levels of attrition (Berman et al., 2009; Safer et al., 2007; Telch et al., 2000, 2001). Both mindfulness-based cognitive therapy (Segal,

Williams, & Teasdale, 2002) and mindfulness-based eating awareness training (Kristeller & Hallett, 1999) have been found to improve binge-eating (Baer et al., 2005a; Baer et al., 2005b; Kristeller & Hallett, 1999). Similar effects have been found with adults and adolescents undergoing modified DBT treatments for AN, bulimia nervosa, and binge-eating disorder (Safer et al., 2007; Safer et al., 2001a, 2001b; Salbach-Andrae et al., 2008; Telch et al., 2000, 2001). Further, early work supports ACT with AN (Heffner et al., 2002), and research findings suggest it may be and have been a useful treatment for adults with AN with a previous history of treatment and protracted course of illness (Berman et al., 2009), a population for which effective treatments are lacking. However, at this point, data are still preliminary and consist only of case studies with simple pre-post test designs limited to short-term follow-ups. Further, there is a need for additional research to determine which components of these interventions are active and responsible for positive outcome.

## Psychological Flexibility as a Process of Change

Although limited, emerging data provide early support for psychological inflexibility as a viable process of change in the treatment of AN. For example, in a study of 21 adults who currently met full diagnostic criteria for AN, 18 adults who met criteria in the past but were currently weight restored, and 23 adults without any history of an eating disorder, we found systematic between-group differences in psychological flexibility. Consistent with the model, individuals with full-syndrome AN reported less psychological flexibility, followed by individuals with a history of the illness who were weight restored, and finally, healthy controls (Merwin, Moskovich, & Zucker, 2010).

Further, in an ongoing treatment study with adolescents with AN[1], our preliminary analyses have indicated that psychological flexibility occurs in tandem with AN symptom remission across treatment. In this randomized controlled trial, adolescents with AN and their caregivers receive 20 sessions of either family or group-based psychotherapy (Zucker, Ferriter, Best, & Brantley, 2005) over the course of 6 months. We assessed eating disorder symptoms and psychological acceptance at baseline, 3 months (mid-treatment), 6 months (end of treatment), and at 9 and 12 months post-intervention follow-up. Of 35 families that were randomized to the study, 18 completed the treatment phase of the study at the time of analysis. We found that psychological inflexibility declined among the adolescents from pre to post-treatment, and throughout the follow-up assessment time points. Change from baseline to 12 months approached significance even in this small sample size. A similar pattern was found for interoceptive deficits, which as defined by the subscale of the Eating Disorder Inventory, includes abilities to label affective experience and the willingness to experience emotional states. Overall, adolescents demonstrated a significant and systematic decline in interoceptive deficits from baseline to follow-up. Interoceptive capabilities are particularly relevant to psychological flexibility because deficits in this area suggest difficulty with ongoing awareness and acceptance of internal states (e.g., hunger/satiety, emotions). Significant improvement in eating disorder symptoms and BMI was observed concurrent to these other changes. Further, time-lagged linear regression analyses indicated that the degree of psychological flexibility (i.e., an adolescent's willingness to experience difficult thoughts and feelings and behave effectively) at one time-point predicted eating disorder symptom severity at the subsequent time point (Merwin, Zucker, Marx, France, & Moskovich, 2009).

We also examined change in the frequency and experience of perfectionistic cognitions as a function of treatment among the adolescents with AN. We expected that while frequency of perfectionistic thoughts might not change as a result of treatment, the extent to which individuals were distressed by these thoughts may. This pattern of results would support targeting how individuals with AN react to their private experience, rather than focusing solely on the content of the cognition. Results supported this conceptualization. Although the frequency of perfectionistic cognitions did not change, adolescents' reported decreased distress in response to these thoughts. Importantly, decreased distress was associated with reductions in dietary restraint and lower global scores on a structured interview of eating disorder symptoms when baseline levels of symptoms were controlled (Zucker et al., in submission). This is consistent with studies of adults with AN that have reported greater acceptance of negative thoughts and feelings about weight and shape corresponded with ED symptom improvement in the absence of any significant change in the content or frequency of the thoughts and feelings themselves (Berman et al., 2009; Heffner et al., 2002).

Together, these studies highlight the potential clinical relevance of psychological flexibility for the prognosis and differentiation of AN from healthy individuals. Lower levels of psychological flexibility distinguish individuals with full syndrome AN from those who are weight restored and healthy controls, while the ability to engage flexibly with distressing thoughts and feelings is associated with AN symptom remission across treatment. Perfectionism and related cognitions which have long been described as part of the phenomenology of AN (Bulik et al., 2003), do not change in frequency but in impact as a result of successful intervention, suggesting how individuals with AN relate to these thoughts may be of prime import. Much additional research is needed to understand how contemporary CBT interventions improve ED symptoms. However, the above data suggest that increased psychological flexibility is a plausible mechanism that warrants further investigation. If tenable, acceptance and mindfulness approaches would be theoretically appropriate. Below we describe some aspects of mindfulness that may be particularly useful in addressing AN as we have conceptualized the illness. Strategies might be delivered either in the context of an acceptance-based treatment package, such as ACT, or provided as adjunct to more traditional cognitive-behavioral therapies.

## Using Mindfulness With AN

The core skill of mindfulness is observing experience as it unfolds in the present moment with full awareness and without unnecessary attachment. In other words, all of experience is greeted openly, which the same degree of curiosity and attentiveness. Experiences are held lightly and enter and exit conscious awareness freely. Mindfulness entails a shift in the frame of reference from one who is guided by the content of thoughts and the intensity and valence of feelings to one who observes these internal experiences. From a mindful stance, an individual recognizes internal events for what they are: dynamic, related to the current and historical situation, and separate and distinct from the individual. This observer stance is characterized by focused, purposeful, and flexible attention to the process of thinking and feeling, rather than the product, content, or valence of cognition and emotion. For example, in a typical mindfulness exercise, an individual may be asked to follow their breath, to notice all sensations that accompany breathing, and to become an unbiased filter of all that transpires internally and externally. When attention is captured by a passing thought e.g., "*I am not doing this right,*" an individual notices that *as a thought* (nothing more, nothing less) and gently guides attention back to the breath. The breath serves as an anchor to the present moment and establishes a connection with the self. At least two things happen during a mindfulness exercise: a) capacities to sustain and shift attention are cultivated, and b) the literal quality of thought is disrupted as the process of thinking is witnessed. Observance and disengagement from the literal properties of thought not only increase behavioral options, but also prevent cognitive elaboration (Bishop et al., 2004). Thoughts can become the object of introspection and the subsequent rationalization, rumination, or other elaboration of thought content that commands attentional capacities that would otherwise be relegated to other aspects of experience and the unfolding present moment. Mindful observation frees these cognitive capacities and allows greater contact with ongoing experience, a requisite for effective action.

## Facilitating a Regulatory Capacity

For individuals with AN, an observer stance may increase capacity to step back from verbal rules and more effectively incorporate somatic-affective experience in decision-making. In this way, mindfulness may cultivate a regulatory capacity in which *experience* can be flexibly integrated with verbal guidelines to direct behavior and produce desirable outcomes. For example, rather than blindly following rules of diet and exercise, individuals with AN can observe these rules *as thoughts* and use their experience to determine whether to comply. In the case of hunger or fatigue, and the rule "*You cannot eat between meals,*" mindfulness skills may be used by the individual with AN to notice the full range of internal and external events, merely observe those aspects that are not helpful, and identify an appropriate behavioral response. Further, because mindfulness promotes approaching all internal experiences with curiosity, openness, and acceptance, using mindfulness may decrease unhelpful secondary reactions, such as fear, guilt, and shame in response to internal experience (e.g., guilt about feelings of satiety). As a result, individuals with AN may be more able to tolerate feelings, and even welcome them as useful information. Over time, through a process of mindful discrimination training, individuals with AN would come into greater contact with the full range of a motivated state and presumably develop capacities to respond effectively. Thus, rather than ignoring or suppressing feelings that are uncertain or uncomfortable, individuals with AN can step back from judgment, take time to determine what, if anything, the feeling is communicating (e.g., the need to eat, the need to seek social support), and respond in a way that allows them to get their physical or emotional needs met. Of importance, flexible attention to internal states has been found to promote more effective behavioral responses among individuals with disordered eating. For example, in a mindfulness-based intervention, increases in satiety awareness were correlated with a reduction in binge-eating episodes (Kristeller & Hallett, 1999). Further, there is at least preliminary data that mindfulness mediates the relationship between anorectic cognition and functioning (Masuda, Price, Anderson, & Wendell, 2010).

## Expanding the Behavioral Repertoire and Improving Social Functioning

Mindfulness allows for an ongoing awareness of all potential candidates to relegate attention and may directly foster the ability to notice and disengage from cues. Thus, rather than attention being captured by a single aspect of experience (e.g., gut discomfort), it may be gently redirected to a multitude of other stimuli, such as awareness of a worry thought, or aspects of the external environment, e.g., other people in the room. For individuals with AN, this may mean that rather than being fixated on how the body feels, they can be aware of how body sensations are related to other internal or external cues, and use this information to guide action. For example, in an evocative social situation, an individual with AN may be fixated on the experience of the gut and unaware that this is associated with anxious arousal related to not being part of a social group. Unaware of the need to be with others, the individual with AN may stay isolated and fixated on the experience of the body. Through flexible attention to the full range of cues, the individual with AN may notice the thought and feeling of being left out, and approach a safe person. With continued practice, flexible attention to fears of rejection and letting go of worry thoughts might enable individuals with AN to approach situations that are of greater risk. In this way, a mindful, observant posture increases the breadth of antecedents available to guide behavior and thus the possibility of novel and diverse responses.

Mindfulness might also expand the breadth of the behavioral repertoire by diminishing the literal or aversive properties of thoughts and feelings which would typically narrow behavior. Because private events are less painful when observed mindfully and thoughts are no longer verbal dictates, an individual has a number of options of how to respond to internal experiences that might otherwise generate avoidance and control. For example, rather than the previous rigid sequence of a knot in stomach, the thought "unacceptable," and then dietary restriction; mindfulness allows alternative responses, such as noticing and accepting the knot in the gut, the ability to observe and describe the accompanying anxious arousal, and the reorienting of attention and behavior to a meaningful life goal (i.e., *"I am experiencing a knot in my gut, and I accept that it is here, and orient to other aspects of my day."*).

A mindful approach might be employed not only with somatic sensations or specific thoughts, but also a collection of private events. For example, a therapist could evoke the experience of *uncertainty* in session and then guide a patient through observing and accepting all aspects of this event. The therapist might begin by facilitating the client simply noticing the experience without acting to make it "go away" or changing it in any way. The client subsequently may be asked to interact with this experience in a number of ways other than avoidance, escape or control (e.g., be curious about it, describe it as an object or a color, etc.). As a result, a repertoire of alternative responses could be fostered such that when *uncertainty* is experienced in the natural environment, behavior can be flexibly organized around the client's life goals. For instance, when confronted with the choice of going to a social event that evokes fears of not knowing what to say or do, an individual with AN might experience strong urges to engage in a clearly prescribed exercise routine instead. Mindfulness practice would help this individual notice this urge, including corresponding thoughts *(i.e., I must exercise)* and feelings (*anxiety*), recognize that it is associated with the social situation, *and* make an active choice to attend. This would require not following the literal dictates of their thoughts and accepting that they will experience fear or discomfort in order to cultivate friendships.

Mindfulness might also facilitate more responsive and potentially enhanced social functioning during the event. For example, in contrast to focusing and attaching to signs of rejection and engaging in elaborative ruminative thought about personal flaws deemed to warrant rejection, an individual with AN might notice thoughts of rejection for what they are (i.e., products of thinking or verbal constructions of the world), and "let go" of these experiences in order to focus attention and resources on the conversation. Over time, this pattern of behavior would be expected to put individuals in contact with positive feedback from others (e.g., warmth, invitations to social events), increasing life value and meaning and decreasing the need for AN.

## Mindfulness and Value-Guided Action

Individuals with AN are reluctant to give up their symptoms, experiencing them as acceptable and in line with their self-conceptualization (Vandereycken, 2006). We propose the reason for this is because symptoms provide a sense of safety amidst confusion and threat, and thus are negatively reinforced. Because the system of starvation is "working," conditions are not conducive to exploring and identifying other life values. As a result, individuals with AN may have limited awareness of things that are meaningful or cared about in a genuine way, other than weight and body. Increasing awareness of moment-to-moment fluctuations in somatic and affective experience and promoting an openness to experience and access to experiential ways of knowing may allow individuals with AN to find other things that are worthwhile and more compelling than their disorder.

Some contemporary approaches specifically work to foster the development of patterns of meaningful action based on individually chosen values as an alternative to avoidance and rigid behavioral control based on thought content. For individuals with AN, values might provide an organizing framework for behavior that allows for the relinquishment of AN. Indeed, without the constraints imposed by AN, the range of behavioral options may be experienced as vast and overwhelming. Values may provide a compass to guide behavior facilitating navigation through this uncertainty. Further, the delineation of values and the corresponding behaviors consistent with these values may motivate approach behaviors. Thus, value-guided exposure to novel or threatening circumstances may be more potent than exposure for the sake of symptom reduction, a finding that may be particularly relevant in a clinical population which is typically behaviorally inhibited and harm avoidant (Cassin & von Ranson, 2005). Further, establishing that particular thoughts and feelings (such as fear of failure) will undoubtedly manifest when individuals work toward things that are important to them (e.g., forming connections with other people), may transform how these internal events are experienced; it is no longer just discomfort, but discomfort with a purpose. An increase in novel and variable behavior may also help to define values not previously realized. Thus, there is greater potential for shaping action that is more adaptive than the current patterns of self-starvation.

## CONCLUSION

## Future Research and Treatment Directions

Individuals with AN are indeed driven to predict and control. Although in certain areas they may have been reinforced for such rigid determination, their failure to sample from unexplored domains and integrate ongoing somatic-affective feedback means ultimately they are not learning optimally: not benefiting from either internal cues or all the environment has to offer and unwilling to risk a solution that may be better (but could be worse). If we are to help those individuals with AN engage fully in their lives, then we may consider integrating mindfulness and acceptance strategies into current treatment models.

The model and predictions outlined above are largely speculative. While mindfulness-based strategies and associated intervention seem theoretically consistent with the deficits and related phenomenology of AN, the evidence base is weak. Such basic considerations as how best to identify and define values in those with AN remain unexplored. Further, within the complex packages that comprise behavioral interventions, the function and efficacy of specific techniques or value of particular philosophical approaches is unknown. The current paper attempts to better characterize the experience of AN to provide a conceptualization of symptom function so novel treatment development can be guided by this framework. Indeed, it is an exciting time for the development of novel interventions for AN. True to the mindful spirit, researchers need to select an approach and unbiasedly observe what unfolds.

## REFERENCES

Baer, R. A., Fischer, S., & Huss, D. B. (2005a). Mindfulness-based cognitive therapy applied to binge eating: A case study. *Cognitive and Behavioral Practice, 12,* 351–358.

Baer, R. A., Fischer, S., & Huss, D. B. (2005b). Mindfulness and acceptance in the treatment of disordered eating. *Journal of Rational-Emotive & Cognitive Behavior Therapy, 23,* 281–300.

Barlow, D. H., Allen, L. B., & Choate, M. L. (2004). Toward a unified treatment for emotional disorders. *Behavior Therapy, 35,* 205–230.

Berkman, N. D., Lohr, K. N., & Bulik, C. M. (2007). Outcomes of eating disorders: A systematic review of the literature. *International Journal of Eating Disorders, 40,* 293–309.

Berman, M. I., Boutelle, K. N., & Crow, S. J. (2009). A case series investigating acceptance and commitment therapy as a treatment for previously treated, unremitted patients with anorexia nervosa. *European Eating Disorders Review, 17*, 426–434.

Bishop, S. R., Lau, M., Shapiro, S., Carlson, L., Anderson, N. D., Carmody, J. . . . Devins, G. (2004). Mindfulness: A proposed operational definition. *Clinical Psychology: Science and Practice, 11*, 230–241.

Bouton, M. E. (1994). Conditioning, temembering, and forgetting. [Review]. *Journal of Experimental Psychology-Animal Behavior Processes, 20*, 219–231.

Bradley, M. M., & Lang, P. J. (2007). Emotion and motivation. In J. T. Cacioppo, L. G. Tassinary & G. G. Berntson (Eds.), *Handbook of psychophysiology* (pp. 581–607). New York, NY: Cambridge University Press.

Broberg, A. G., Hjalmers, I., & Nevonen, L. (2001). Eating disorders, attachment and interpersonal difficulties: A comparison between 18-to 24-year-old patients and normal controls. *European Eating Disorders Review, 9*, 381–396.

Bruch, H. (1973). *Eating disorders: Obesity, anorexia nervosa and the person within.* New York, NY: Basic Books.

Brumberg, J. J. (1985). "Fasting girls": Reflections on writing the history of anorexia nervosa. *Monographs of the Society for Research in Child Development, 50*(4/5), 93–104.

Brumberg, J. J. (1988). *Fasting girls: The emergence of anorexia nervosa as a modern disease*: Cambridge, MA: Harvard University Press.

Bulik, C. M., Berkman, N. D., Brownley, K. A., Sedway, J. A., & Lohr, K. N. (2007). Anorexia nervosa treatment: A systematic review of randomized controlled trials. *International Journal of Eating Disorders, 40*, 310–320.

Bulik, C. M., Tozzi, F., Anderson, C., Mazzeo, S., Aggen, S., & Sullivan, P. F. (2003). The relation between components of perfectionism and eating disorders. *American Journal of Psychiatry, 160*, 366–368.

Cassin, S. E., & von Ranson, K. M. (2005). Personality and eating disorders: A decade in review. *Clinical Psychology Review, 25*, 895–916.

Craig, A. D. (2004). Human feelings: why are some more aware than others? *Trends in Cognitive Sciences, 8*, 239–241.

Eddy, K. T., Dorer, D. J., Franko, D. L., Tahilani, K., Thompson-Brenner, H., & Herzog, D. B. (2008). Diagnostic crossover in anorexia nervosa and bulimia nervosa: Implications for DSM-V. *The American Journal of Psychiatry, 165*, 245–250.

Eisler, I., Simic, M., Russell, G. F. M., & Dare, C. (2007). A randomised controlled treatment trial of two forms of family therapy in adolescent anorexia nervosa: A five-year follow-up. *Journal of Child Psychology and Psychiatry, 48*, 552–560.

Forbes, E. E., & Dahl, R. E. (2010). Pubertal development and behavior: Hormonal activation of social and motivational tendencies. *Brain and Cognition, 72*(1), 66–72.

Godart, N. T., Flament, M. F., Curt, F., Perdereau, F., Lang, F., Venisse, J. L. . . . Fermanian, J. (2003). Anxiety disorders in subjects seeking treatment for eating disorders: a DSM-IV controlled study. *Psychiatry Research, 117*, 245–258.

Godart, N. T., Flament, M. F., Perdereau, F., & Jeammet, P. (2002). Comorbidity between eating disorders and anxiety disorders: A review. *International Journal of Eating Disorders, 32*, 253–270.

Goodwin, R. D., & Fitzgibbon, M. L. (2002). Social anxiety as a barrier to treatment for eating disorders. *International Journal of Eating Disorders, 32*, 103–106.

Gross, J. J., & Levenson, R. W. (1997). Hiding feelings: The acute effects of inhibiting negative and positive emotion. *Journal of Abnormal Psychology, 106*, 95–103.

Halmi, K. A., Sunday, S. R., Strober, M., Kaplan, A., Woodside, D. B., Fichter, M. . . . Kaye, W. H. (2000). Perfectionism in anorexia nervosa: Variation by clinical subtype, obsessionality, and pathological eating behavior. *The American Journal of Psychiatry, 157*, 1799–1805.

Harris, J. A., & Benedict, F. F. (1919). *A biometric study of basal metabolism in man.* Washington, DC: Carnegie Institution of Washington.

Hayes, L. J., Thompson, S., & Hayes, S. C. (1989). Stimulus equivalence and rule following. *Journal of the Experimental Analysis of Behavior, 52*, 275–291.

Hayes, S. C., Brownstein, A. J., Haas, J. R., & Greenway, D. E. (1986). Instructions, multiple schedules, and extinction: Distinguishing rule-governed from schedule-controlled behavior. *Journal of the Experimental Analysis of Behavior, 46*, 137–147.

Hayes, S. C., Brownstein, A. J., Zettle, R. D., & Rosenfarb, I. (1986). Rule-governed behavior and sensitivity to changing consequences of responding. *Journal of the Experimental Analysis of Behavior, 45*, 237–256.

Hayes, S. C., Wilson, K. G., Gifford, E. V., Follette, V. M., & Strosahl, K. (1996). Experiential avoidance and behavioral disorders: A functional dimensional approach to diagnosis and treatment. *Journal of Consulting and Clinical Psychology, 64*, 1152–1168.

Heffner, M., Sperry, J., Eifert, G. H., & Detweiler, M. (2002). Acceptance and commitment therapy in the treatment of an adolescent female with anorexia nervosa: A case example. *Cognitive and Behavioral Practice, 9*, 232–236.

Herpertz-Dahlmann, B., Müller, B., Herpertz, S., Heussen, N., Hebebrand, J., & Remschmidt, H. (2001). Prospective 10-year follow-up in adolescent anorexia nervosa: Course, outcome, psychiatric comorbidity, and psychosocial adaptation. *Journal of Child Psychology and Psychiatry, 42*, 603–612.

Hudson, J. I., Hiripi, E., Pope, H. G., Jr., & Kessler, R. C. (2007). The prevalence and correlates of eating disorders in the National Comorbidity Survey Replication. *Biological Psychiatry, 61*, 348–358.

Kaye, W. H., Bulik, C. M., Thornton, L., Barbarich, N., & Masters, K. (2004). Comorbidity of anxiety disorders with anorexia and bulimia nervosa. *The American Journal of Psychiatry, 161*, 2215–2221.

Kaye, W. H., Fudge, J. L., & Paulus, M. (2009). New insights into symptoms and neurocircuit function of anorexia nervosa. [10.1038/nrn2682]. *Nature Reviews Neuroscience, 10*, 573–584.

Keel, P. K., & Haedt, A. (2008). Evidence-based psychosocial treatments for eating problems and eating disorders. *Journal of Clinical Child and Adolescent Psychology, 37*, 39–61.

Kristeller, J. L., & Hallett, C. B. (1999). An exploratory study of a meditation-based intervention for binge eating disorder. *Journal of Health Psychology, 4*, 357–363.

Lilenfeld, L. R. R., Wonderlich, S., Riso, L. P., Crosby, R., & Mitchell, J. (2006). Eating disorders and personality: A methodological and empirical review. *Clinical Psychology Review, 26*, 299–320.

Lock, J., & Fitzpatrick, K. K. (2009). Advances in psychotherapy for children and adolescents with eating disorders. *American Journal of Psychotherapy, 63,* 287–303.

Masuda, A., Price, M., Anderson, P. L., & Wendell, J. W. (2010). Disordered eating-related cognition and psychological flexibility as predictors of psychological health among college students. *Behavior Modification, 34*(1), 3–15.

Mathers, C. D., Vos, E. T., Stevenson, C. E., & Begg, S. J. (2000). The Australian burden of disease study: measuring the loss of health from diseases, injuries and risk factors. *Medical Journal of Australia, 172,* 592–596.

Merwin, R. M., Moskovich, A. A., & Zucker, N. L. (2010, November). *Dietary restraint as a maladaptive emotion regulation strategy among individuals with anorexia nervosa.* Paper presented at the annual meeting of the Association for Behavioral and Cognitive Therapies, San Francisco, CA.

Merwin, R. M., Rosenthal, M. Z., & Coffey, K. A. (2009). Experiential avoidance mediates the relationship between sexual victimization and psychological symptoms: Replicating findings in an ethnically diverse sample. *Cognitive Research and Therapy, 33,* 537–542.

Merwin, R. M., Zucker, N. L., Lacy, J. L., & Elliott, C. A. (2010). Interoceptive awareness in eating disorders: Distinguishing lack of clarity from non-acceptance of internal experience. *Cognition and Emotion, 24,* 872–902. .

Merwin, R. M., Zucker, N. L., Marx, L., France, B. E., & Moskovich, A. A. (2009, November). *Acceptance of internal experience as a mechanism of change in the treatment of anorexia nervosa.* Paper presented at the Association for Behavioral and Cognitive Therapies, New York, NY.

Miller, S. P., Redlich, A. D., & Steiner, H. (2003). The stress response in anorexia nervosa. *Child Psychiatry & Human Development, 33,* 295–306.

Mitchell, J. E., & Crow, S. (2006). Medical complications of anorexia nervosa and bulimia nervosa. *Current Opinion in Psychiatry, 19,* 438–443.

Raney, T. J., Thornton, L. M., Berrettini, W., Brandt, H., Crawford, S., Fichter, M. M. . . . Bulik, C.M. (2008). Influence of overanxious disorder of childhood on the expression of anorexia nervosa. *International Journal of Eating Disorders, 41,* 326–332.

Safer, D. L., Lock, J., & Couturier, J. L. (2007). Dialectical behavior therapy modified for adolescent binge eating disorder: A case report. *Cognitive and Behavioral Practice, 14,* 157–167.

Safer, D. L., Telch, C. F., & Agras, W. S. (2001a). Dialectical behavior therapy adapted for bulimia: A case report. *International Journal of Eating Disorders, 30,* 101–106.

Safer, D. L., Telch, C. F., & Agras, W. S. (2001b). Dialectical behavior therapy for bulimia nervosa. *The American Journal of Psychiatry, 158,* 632–634.

Salbach-Andrae, H., Bohnekamp, I., Pfeiffer, E., Lehmkuhl, U., & Miller, A. L. (2008). Dialectical behavior therapy of anorexia and bulimia nervosa among adolescents: A case series. *Cognitive and Behavioral Practice, 15,* 415–425.

Schmidt, U., & Treasure, J. (2006). Anorexia nervosa: Valued and visible. A cognitive-interpersonal maintenance model and its implications for research and practice. *British Journal of Clinical Psychology, 45,* 343–366.

Segal, Z. V., Williams, J. M. G., & Teasdale, J. D. (2002). *Mindfulness-based cognitive therapy for depression: A new approach to preventing relapse.* New York, NY: Guilford Press.

Serpell, L., Treasure, J., Teasdale, J., & Sullivan, V. (1999). Anorexia nervosa: Friend or foe? *International Journal of Eating Disorders, 25,* 177–186.

Steinglass, J., & Walsh, B. T. (2006). Habit learning and anorexia nervosa: A cognitive neuroscience hypothesis. *International Journal of Eating Disorders, 39,* 267–275.

Steinglass, J. E., Walsh, B. T., & Stern, Y. (2006). Set shifting deficit in anorexia nervosa. *Journal of the International Neuropsychological Society, 12,* 431–435.

Striegel-Moore, R. H., & Bulik, C. M. (2007). Risk factors for eating disorders. *American Psychologist, 62,* 181–198.

Strober, M., Freeman, R., Lampert, C., & Diamond, J. (2007). The association of anxiety disorders and obsessive compulsive personality disorder with anorexia nervosa: Evidence from a family study with discussion of nosological and neurodevelopmental implications. *International Journal of Eating Disorders, 40*(Supl), S46–S51.

Tchanturia, K., Morris, R. G., Anderluh, M. B., Collier, D. A., Nikolaou, V., & Treasure, J. (2004). Set shifting in anorexia nervosa: An examination before and after weight gain, in full recovery and relationship to childhood and adult OCPD traits. *Journal of Psychiatric Research, 38,* 545–552.

Telch, C. F., Agras, W. S., & Linehan, M. M. (2000). Group dialectical behavior therapy for binge-eating disorder: A preliminary, uncontrolled trial. *Behavior Therapy, 31,* 569–582.

Telch, C. F., Agras, W. S., & Linehan, M. M. (2001). Dialectical behavior therapy for binge eating disorder. *Journal of Consulting and Clinical Psychology, 69*(6), 1061–1065.

Tozzi, F., Thornton, L. M., Klump, K. L., Fichter, M. M., Halmi, K. A., Kaplan, A. S. . . . Kaye, W.H. (2005). Symptom fluctuation in eating disorders: Correlates of diagnostic crossover. *The American Journal of Psychiatry, 162,* 732–740.

Vandereycken, W. (2006). Denial of illness in anorexia nervosa—A conceptual review: Part 1 diagnostic significance and assessment. *European Eating Disorders Review, 14,* 341–351.

Wagner, A., Aizenstein, H., Venkatraman, V. K., Fudge, J., May, J. C., Mazurkewicz, L. . . . Kaye, W.H. (2007). Altered reward processing in women recovered from anorexia nervosa. *The American Journal of Psychiatry, 164,* 1842–1849.

Wang, T., Hung, C. C. Y., & Randall, D. J. (2006). The comparative physiology of food deprivation: From feast to famine. *Annual Review of Physiology, 68*(1), 223–251.

Wentz, E., Gillberg, I. C., Anckarsater, H., Gillberg, C., & Rastam, M. (2009). Adolescent-onset anorexia nervosa: 18-year outcome. *British Journal of Psychiatry, 194,* 168–174.

Wildes, J. E., Ringham, R. M., & Marcus, M. D. (2010). Emotion avoidance in patients with anorexia nervosa: Initial test of a functional model. *International Journal of Eating Disorders, 43,* 398–404.

Wilson, G. T., Grilo, C. M., & Vitousek, K. M. (2007). Psychological treatment of eating disorders. *American Psychologist, 62*, 199–216.

Wilson, K. G., & Hayes, S. C. (1996). Resurgence of derived stimulus relations. *Journal of the Experimental Analysis of Behavior, 66*, 267–281.

Wulfert, E., Greenway, D. E., Farkas, P., & Hayes, S. C. (1994). Correlation between self-reported rigidity and rule-governed insensitivity to operant contingencies. *Journal of Applied Behavior Analysis, 27*, 659–671.

Zucker, N. L., Ferriter, C., Best, S., & Brantley, A. (2005). Group parent training: A novel approach for the treatment of eating disorders. *Eating Disorders, 13*, 391–405.

Zucker, N., Merwin, R. M., Moskovich, A. A., Konrad Ingle, K., Bulik, C. M., & Lock, J. (in submission). Changes in perfectionistic cognition over the course of treatment in adolescents with anorexia nervosa.

Zucker, N. L., Losh, M., Bulik, C. M., LaBar, K. S., Piven, J., & Pelphrey, K. A. (2007). Anorexia nervosa and autism spectrum disorders: Guided investigation of social cognitive endophenotypes. *Psychological Bulletin, 133*, 976–1006.

# Thinking Through the Body: The Conceptualization of Yoga as Therapy for Individuals With Eating Disorders

LAURA DOUGLASS

*Interdisciplinary Educational Studies Program, Lesley University,*
*Cambridge, Massachusetts, USA*

*Yoga has historically been viewed as a discipline that increases self--awareness through body based practices, meditation, self-study, and the reading of philosophical texts. In the 21st century the mindfulness techniques of yoga have been adapted as an adjunct to the treatment of individuals with eating disorders. In an effort to understand the conceptualization of yoga as therapy for individuals with eating disorders, this article juxtaposes how mindfulness based yoga is regarded in three disciplines: sociology, neuroscience, and the "spiritual texts" of yoga.*

## INTRODUCTION

The body vividly expresses our differences. Through gestures, facial movements and somatic expressions, the body makes explicit our physical ability, age, ethnicity, and many of our emotions and thoughts (Shusterman, 2006). Understanding what the body communicates and needs is central to the concerns of those with eating disorders. While most clinicians would agree that they are committed to facilitating learning through and about the body, it is extremely difficult to design a residential curriculum that engages the body in healthy ways. Consciously or unconsciously, each aspect of treatment addresses the body: regular walks, regulation of food, monitoring of bathrooms, time for dance, music, or other forms of art, and relaxation. In an effort to more explicitly address embodiment, some clinical directors are adding the practice of yoga to their mental health programs (Boudette, 2006; Douglass, 2009; Lavey et al., 2005).

Only a few studies support the efficacy of yoga for eating disorders and at least one study has shown that yoga has no effect at all (McIver, O'Halloran, & McGartland, 2009; Mitchell, Mazzeo, Rausch, & Cooke, 2007; Scime & Cook-Cottone, 2008). In part, clinical directors are choosing to include yoga as an adjunct to existing treatment based on studies which support its effectiveness for illnesses like OCD, PTSD, depression, and anxiety; disorders that often co-exist with eating disorders (da Silva, Ravindran, & Ravindran, 2009; Shannahoff-Khalsa, 2004; Sharma, Das, Mondal, Goswami, & Gandhi, 2006). The decision to include yoga as an adjunct to treatment may also be based on contemporary psychological texts that are increasingly placing primacy on the body as a modality of healing or on yoga's intimate interrelationship with other mindfulness based therapies (Ogden, Minton, & Pain, 2006; Rothschild, 2000; Salmon, Lush, Jablonski, & Sephton, 2009). Indeed, the justification to include yoga in residential programs is informed by multiple sources, reflecting that our current understanding of yoga is created by a confluence of personal, historical, popular, and academic sources.

Yoga has yet to be fixed by history and thus suffers (and benefits) from looseness (Alter, 2009). In this article I juxtapose how mindfulness based yoga is conceptualized by three disciplines: sociology, neuroscience, and the "spiritual texts" of yoga. Being aware of how and when these divergent disciplines inform my conceptualization of yoga significantly contributes to my own understanding of the limitations and strengths of my role as an educator within the clinical setting. Each discipline that I draw on to make sense of yoga is embedded with its own distinctive cultural assumptions about embodiment. In residential settings, these assumptions become unspoken components by which the individual evaluates the ways in which they use their body. Making the assumptions explicit is important because the practices we engage our bodies in throughout the day reflect what we think is important, what we think we "should" do, and what we think we are capable of.

## WHAT IS MINDFUL YOGA?

In North America yoga is primarily associated with a series of physical postures, yet it can also include complex theories of human learning and psychology (Dalal, 2001a; Krishnamurti, 2003). The teaching of yoga is extremely eclectic, but one important commonality is the use of yoga practices to achieve freedom from the way we habitually interpret the world. Mindful yoga is primarily interested in raising an individual's awareness of the patterns of his or her mind; it does this through postures, breathing practices, deep relaxation, and concentration techniques. Mindful yoga can be a powerful tool through which we encounter our inner lives and begin to understand its effect on our embodied experience. For example, in a mindful yoga class students might rest between each yoga posture to gauge whether they are more comfortable with movement or rest. They become familiar with their own particular mental responses to "rest," and are asked if there are any adjustments they can make (either physically or mentally) to be at ease in both action and inaction. By experimenting with mental responses to something as simple as "rest," the student begins to experience how different types of thoughts actually feel different within the body. Bodily sensations are known to influence our cognitive decision making, thought processes, and body image (Babu et al., 2002; Ogden et al., 2006). Mindful yoga classes are an opportunity for students to learn how to discriminate between "bodily sensations" and "thoughts." Understanding that there are multiple reactions to a single sensation can provide some individuals with an essential tool to work with their eating disorder: choice.

The group yoga classes I teach may have unexpected therapeutic benefits: better ability to sleep, improved digestion, and increased ability to relax, handle stress or tolerate emotion. Yet the idea that thinking which is grounded in the body is "therapeutic" as opposed to "educational" is related to a deeply entrenched philosophical separation of the mind from the body, now infamously known as "Descartes Error" (Damasio, 1999). I do not see the yoga classes I teach as "therapeutic" for my goal is not to provide or assist in a cure. I teach embodied learning. Together, the clients and I systematically engage in the process and action of thinking through the body.

As a practitioner of yoga since 1995, I have a felt sense that the practice of mindful yoga helps me move from "thinking about" states of mind to, literally, "embodying" new ways of thinking. Despite my experience, it is important that I not impose my own learning on individuals with eating disorders; they may experience embodiment in completely different ways. Mindful yoga is not prescriptive, but a form of inquiry into how we, as individuals, experience the interplay between our thoughts and our bodies. Mindful yoga calls for the *negotiation* and the *embrace* of multiple meaning over any one single vision of reality. In some ways, accepting multiple meanings is what embodiment is all about. In *Philosophy in the flesh: The embodied mind and its challenges to Western thought*, the authors state:

> Embodied truth requires us to give up the illusion that there exists a unique correct description of any situation. Because of the multiple levels of our embodiment, there is no one level at which one can express all the truths we can know about a given subject matter. But even if there is no *one* correct description, there can still be many correct descriptions, depending on our embodied understandings at different levels or from different perspectives. (Lakoff & Johnson, 1999, p. 109)

## SOCIOLOGY—HOW CONTEXT IMPACTS EMBODIMENT

For sociologists, embodiment usually refers to the process by which the body becomes a vehicle for socialization (Bourdieu & Passeron, 2000; Shapiro, 1999). For example, the average person in a residential setting receives positive regard for not moving (movement may be described as "disrupting") and bathroom breaks are frequently regulated. This regulation provides a sense of safety that is essential for those struggling with eating disorders, as unregulated time becomes a temptation to purge a recent meal or exercise. Despite the compassionate necessity of such regulation, the cultural message is that the body should be subordinate to both the mind and authorities. Disciplining the body that cannot "sit still" or that "compulsively exercises" unconsciously teaches that the body, when not controlled, leads to alienation and suffering. It is necessary to help individuals with eating disorders understand that some of their actions consistently lead to suffering. As a yoga teacher one of my goals is to broaden the sociological conception of the body from something that must be "disciplined," to an integral part of the self that needs to be listened to, cared for, and communicated with.

A central paradox of residential treatment settings is that they both mirror the societal expectation that individuals should control their bodies (as is evidenced in the regulation of walks, bathroom breaks, etc.) and encouragement for individuals to question this societal norm (as is evidenced in the inclusion of yoga, other mindfulness techniques, and therapy). Mindfulness in the clinical setting requires recognizing such ambiguities and helping individuals who may have a rigid way of conceptualizing embodiment relate to the multiple, and sometimes contradictory, ways in which people think about body. The curricula of residential programs reflect our culture's unconscious and conscious hopes, frustrations, assumptions and contradictions about embodiment. Educator Ross states that the body ". . . has been absorbing lessons we weren't even aware were being taught. Responding in ways direct and obvious and hidden and recondite, it has shown itself as a product . . . few were aware was being produced" (Ross, as quotedin Peters et al., 2004, p. 169). Whether or not we address our assumptions, the body is always present and learning.

### The Privatization of Stress

Underlying the presence of yoga in the clinical setting is the 21st century discourse which imagines the "self" as stressed and envisions therapeutic spaces in which this stress can be handled (Hoyez, 2007). Practitioners of yoga often capitalize on this dominant discourse by referring to the practices of yoga as a set of "stress management" and "self-care" tools (Kelly & Colquhoun, 2005). The practices of yoga do seem particularly effective in assisting individuals to handle stress; in fact, stress reduction is one of the most consistent findings in yoga related research (Brown & Gerbarg, 2005; Smith, Hancock, Blake-Mortimer, & Eckert, 2007). The integration of progressive relaxation (*yoga nidra*) and breathing practices (*pranayama*) into the mindful yoga classes I teach are intended to help the individual experience how cultivating self-awareness and self-care can positively impact their lives. The group yoga class is a safe environment in which the clients, themselves, learn to recognize what does and does not elicit the relaxation response. The same individual may experience a breathing practice as profoundly relaxing one day and intensely irritating the next. The reasons for this shift in experience are varied; a particularly persistent negative thought, gas, abdominal cramps, new medication, or a simple shift in the teacher's voice can all influence the embodied experience. Seeing how one's own thoughts and visceral reactions shift the experience of a yoga practice may help the individual have insight into their inner lives and their own personal response to internal and external stressors.

As a yoga teacher, I am concerned with how an individual thinks about the experience of stress and how it feels within the body. I am also concerned with the way in which individuals embody unquestioned cultural assumptions about stress and wellness. Clients, clinicians, and yoga teachers alike may see the value of using yoga to manage stress, but it may be unrealistic to assume that every individual can handle the multiple pressures of society, family, school, and work. Imagining that it is the "self" alone which experiences and must manage stress contributes to the creation of a societal context in which a "profound burden of responsibility" is placed on the individual (Kelly & Colquhoun, 2003, p. 201). We must question whether our culture's emphasis on the individual management of stress serves to take the responsibility off of the larger cultural intuitions which generate stress in the first place. Researchers are beginning to question what makes it possible, at this moment in history, to link success with the management of stress (Kelly & Colquhoun, 2003).

Some studies show that adding educational classes on the sociological issues that may contribute to the high rise in eating disorders within affluent societies may be helpful in preventing the disorder (Scime, Cook-Cottone, Kane, & Watson, 2006; Seid et al., 1994). From a sociological perspective, untangling the intimate relationship between self, society and eating disorders is imperative; it is seen as the missing link to understanding the "modern disease" of eating disorders. Of course, relying on sociological constructs to describe mental illness is controversial. If taken to an extreme, this approach can inadvertently downplay the role that neurobiology has in the etiology of the disorder. In 2001, when Harvard University opened its Brain Imaging Center, my interest in the sociological constructs of eating disorders was momentarily replaced by an enthusiasm that neuroscience could, finally, reveal why (or if) mindfulness was effective for those with eating disorders.

# NEUROSCIENCE: THE BIOLOGY BEHIND YOGA IN THE CLINICAL SETTING

Neurobiologists view embodiment quite differently than sociologists; here embodiment is specifically related to the biology of the human experience. Recent findings in neuroscience confirm that the body is essential to all forms of learning (Zull et al., 2006). Neurobiologists now view the mind as an inseparable aspect of the body—a view long held in the yogic traditions of psychology (Dalal, 2001a). For example, cortisol, an important hormone to help individuals deal with stress, is produced in excess for those under chronic stress. This is particularly troublesome for individuals with eating disorders, as prolonged high cortisol levels are known to have many adverse physiological and mental symptoms. These include: lowered immunity, decreased bone density, decreased muscle tissue, and poor cognitive functioning. The somatic practices of yoga are now recommended by many physicians because the regular practice of yoga has consistently been shown to reduce cortisol levels (Carlson, Speca, Patel, & Goodey, 2004; Granath, Ingvarsson, von Thiele, & Lundberg, 2006; West, Otte, Geher, Johnson, & Mohr, 2004). Neuroscience has become an increasingly popular discipline to help explain mindfulness based practices as it seems to offer body-based rationale for what clinicians know intuitively (Siegel, 2010).

## Interoception and the Practice of Yoga

We learn about ourselves through movement not only "of" the body, but "in" the body. When we come in contact with our environment the interior of the body is constantly changing: hormonal shifts, digestion, movement of fluids, ligament, and bone. These sensations are the result of "interoceptors" or sensory nerve receptors "that receive and transmit sensations from stimuli originating in the interior of the body" (Ogden et al., 2006, p. 15). For example, in a yoga class information is received by the brain from the muscles and joints (called proprioception) as a result of sensory receptors that are sensitive to stretch or pressure in the tissue that surrounds them (Bundy, Lane, & Murray, 2002). Yoga instructors attempt to help students understand and interpret the different sensations they are experiencing by giving verbal cues as to what may be transpiring in the body; this type of learning is called interoceptive.

One of the most effective means I have found for quieting a particularly restless client in the yoga classes I teach is to engage interoceptive learning. I do this by engaging the student's mind in the physiological sensations of a yoga posture that relieves pressure in the abdomen (many of our clients suffer from gas, constipation, and cramping and desire some relief from these negative sensations). For example, in *setu bandhasana* or bridge pose, students lie on their back and bring their feet close to their hips. Pressing their feet into the floor, they lift their hips from the ground. I follow this movement with the suggestion that they let their hips drop down one inch from their highest position and reach their knees to the front wall. This lengthening of the abdominal cavity creates a perceived sense of "space" and "lightness" that 1) teaches individuals they have some control over interoceptive stimuli, and 2) in the short moment in which they are holding the pose and exploring interoception, they are experiencing the present moment fully, free of critical thinking or a mind-set that habitually moves to the past or future.

Knowledge of interoceptive experiences has been shown to play a potential role in anxiety management, prevention of panic attacks and the prevention of substance abuse (Goldberg, 2001; Meuret, Ritz, Wilhelm, & Roth, 2005; Wald & Taylor, 2008). Many of these illnesses coincide with eating disorders, but I found no research that specifically addresses the role of interoceptive learning for those with eating disorders. Existing research does confirm that yoga classes preformed slowly and with awareness are more effective at dealing with stress (Agte & Chiplonkar, 2008; Michalsen et al., 2005). Neuroscientists recognize that individuals can and do improve their perceptual and motor skills, as well as their knowledge of interoceptive stimuli (Kaas in Babu et al., 2002; Bundy et al., 2002).

The discipline of neuroscience gives primacy to the body because it is a concrete way in which to think about our experience. Understanding how neuroscientists think about embodiment has helped me to have a more sophisticated way of articulating and thinking about what is happening in my mindful yoga classes. Current research on yoga also helps me explain the benefits and contraindications of yoga to clinicians and students. Yet as someone who works with individuals who have eating disorders, I hesitate to completely adopt the perspectives offered by neuroscience. The perspectives of neuroscience are useful, clear, and even beautiful; however, I am often led to think that if only I "do this or that" with the body it will alleviate suffering. That is, once again I have unconsciously adopted a theory that believes if only the body can be manipulated in the "right" way, healing will occur. It is the unquestioning acceptance of this belief about the body that led me to explore some of the more philosophical approaches to healing found in the traditional literature and teachings of yoga.

## YOGA: CREATING MEANING OUT OF SUFFERING

When considering the role of yoga within a residential program for individuals with eating disorders it is important to reflect on the fact that yoga was never intended to treat illness. Yogic theories of psychology are concerned with how to reach our full human potential (Dalal, 2001a, 2001b). Yogic philosophy cannot replace the necessity of proper nutrition, medication, psychotherapy, or family counseling for individuals with eating disorders. The aim of yoga is to understand the nature of regular human suffering, which is often overlaid on top of, or underneath, eating disorders. The value of yoga psychology is that it does not concern itself with the physiological symptoms of disease (the body itself), but with illness—the human experience, or meaning making, about the disease (Desikachar & Cravens, 1998). These theories rarely make their way into my group yoga classes, which are designed to focus primarily on introducing the somatic practices of yoga (postures, breathing practices, and progressive relaxation). They have, however, been quintessential to my own conceptualization of yoga's place within the residential setting.

There are many yogic texts, but I will focus on the *Aittreya* and *Taittreya Upanishads,* which were composed between 1100–700 BCE (Radakrishna, 1998). While yogic theory recognizes the role of nourishing the physical body, this literature also points to the importance of nourishing ourselves with relationships, knowledge, and service to others (Sankaracharya, Suresvaracharya, & Vidyaranya, 1993). According to the *Aittreya* and *Taittreya Upanishads,* part of the human experience is to be born with an intense desire for satisfaction and happiness. In an effort to satiate our deep yearning, we search for satisfaction in relationships, possessions, and position. Often, we achieve the object of our desire only to find that it did not bring lasting happiness. It is the perpetual search for happiness outside of ourselves that later yogic texts would describe as *avidya,* or the basic ignorance which brings us suffering (Satchidananda, 2003). The *Taittreya Upanishads* offers a complex theory of five *koshas,* or false impressions, that veil our innate happiness. In this article I will focus solely on the first of the five koshas: *anamaya,* or the physical sense of self.

## The Physical Sense of Self, *Anamaya Kosha*

The physical body, or *anamaya kosha,* is recognized as important because it solidifies our identity. The difficulty, according to yogic texts, is when we begin to solely identify with the body as the sum of who we are. The more we identify with the body, the more we believe that other people cannot ever truly understand one another; you and I are different. Predictably, this line of thinking leads to a sense of isolation that is difficult to penetrate because relationship is not seen as a viable option that leads to satisfaction (Krishnananda, 2009). The individual turns their desire for satisfaction, time and time again, to what does seem viable: "fixing" the body, even when there is nothing wrong with it. What is wrong, from a yogic perspective, is that our deeper yearning for wholeness and relationship is not satisfied. According to the *Upanishads* the fundamental question for all humans, not just those with eating disorders, is for what are we really hungering? (Krishnananda, 2009).

The second difficulty in over-identifying with the body, according to the *Upanishads*, is that the individual suffers from an unconscious fear of death (Sankaracharya et al., 1993). This fear is avoided in three fundamental and predictable ways: endless attention to the body (massage, exercise, facials); dulling of the senses (through alcohol or over/under eating); or an attempt to grasp and control the minute details of life (Krishnananda, 2009). Eventually, the individual may begin to recognize that engagement in these activities is not moving them toward satisfaction, but to a deeper entanglement with suffering. It is at this point that many individuals attempt to live a quieter life, to engage in mindfulness, or other spiritual practices in an effort to "get rid" of suffering. According to the *Upanishads,* this effort is all too often usurped by a long to-do list that supports the idea that we, our physical presence, is wanted. How do we, as individuals, escape this nagging yearning for satisfaction? The *Upanishads* share that it is the human attempt to "get rid" of suffering that is false. We cannot toss our suffering aside, we must nourish it. We must care for and attempt to understand the suffering which comes to us. Yoga, which means "yoke" or "unite," is intended to bring together all aspects of our selves, including our frailty and afflictions.

The *Upanishads* do not outline a theory for individuals with mental illness, but attempts to offer insight into the human experience. The goal of yoga is to learn to be free in the midst of immense suffering and to nourish, not fix, what is wrong. I find this reframing to be pivotal to the small work that I do teaching yoga in a residential center. Stepping out of the melodramas evoked by the illness of eating disorders is not easy. I am often tempted to move into a critical state of mind that rejects the possibility of any good that I can accomplish with the simple somatic practices of yoga. Certainly, yoga alone cannot "fix" what is wrong with people who find themselves wrestling with the complexities of eating disorders, but the *Upanishads* offer me, as a teacher, freedom from the necessity to fix anything. What it asks me to do is to nourish; to see that affliction exists and to create a space in which suffering is a welcome part of the human experience. This slight shift in meaning making (from fixing to nourishing) allows me to see the residential setting as an opportunity for these individuals to be nourished by the counselors, therapists, social workers, art therapists, nutritionists, and yoga educators who work with them. The residential setting is an opportunity to see that we (the treatment team and clients) are not that different. We can understand one another.

The group yoga class I teach in the residential setting is not explicitly about meaning making. In part, this is because meaning making is deeply personal. It may be helpful for me, as a yoga teacher, to conceptualize the "problem" of eating disorders as one of consumption: which opportunities to accept, which to reject; which relationships to nourish, which to let go of; which cultural messages should we embody, which to ignore. It would be arrogant to impose this, or any meaning on those who attend my group classes. I do not know how yoga, as an embodied way of knowing, clashes with the existing discourse(s) around the body held by individuals in the residential program. Certainly, there is an implicit meaning in the group yoga classes I teach: it is safe to relax, it is okay to respond to the sensations of the body (adjusting or coming out of the poses altogether).

Viewing eating disorders with philosophy (instead of with the multiple lenses of neurobiology, psychology, and sociology) is too simplistic. It also contains several very serious dangers. One of the hazards is the possibility that some individuals will view people with eating disorders as responsible for creating their disorder, independent of biology. Or that the disorder is "simply" one of meaning making. Meaning making is not simple. The creation of meaning is one of the most significant ways in which we express our individuality and humanity. It is the social worker or therapist's role to help those with eating disorders unlock the meaning that they believe their eating disorder holds; yet the need to finding meaning in tragedy is not something unique to those with eating disorders, but something which they have in common with the rest of humanity.

## CONCLUSION

As humans we have a visceral knowledge that when we change what we do with and to our bodies, our experience changes. What we eat, the medications we take, how we exercise or relax all impacts our embodied experience—how we feel. It is the primacy I give to my embodied experience that leads me to rely on neuroscience as offering the most significant conceptualization of mindfulness practices. While research is just beginning that aims to determine yoga's specific place in mental health settings, embodied mindfulness techniques are clearly relevant to the extent that they align with contemporary models of cognition and learning. The exact mechanisms by which yoga practices enhance learning has yet to be worked out. There is a genuine need for a cohesive model that explains the complex way in which yoga should and should not be integrated into the treatment of individuals with eating disorders.

If neuroscience develops a clear conceptualization of yoga's effectiveness for those with eating disorders, it still may not hold all the answers. Each human experience of suffering is a unique and disordered confluence of biological distress, personality, and cultural demands colliding to create feelings of isolation, fear, and terror. As someone who is interested in understanding yoga within the context of a residential program for people with eating disorders, the work that I do is, of necessity, interdisciplinary. I cross traditional boundaries of "disciplines" and combine schools of thought in an effort to solve or understand the problems which arise in my classes. The irony of rejecting a specific "discipline" as holding the key to conceptualizing mindful yoga for individuals with eating disorders has not escaped me. Individuals with eating disorders wrestle with the concept of discipline all the time; when do they provide regulation and order? When punishment, correction and control? Recognizing that this paradox is inherent to all disciplines may help us to find the unstated assumptions underlining our work.

Interdisciplinarity cannot provide the incisive insights of sociology, the detailed research of neuroscience, or the philosophy of yoga; each of these disciplines has specialists with very specific ways of making meaning and generating knowledge. Every discipline requires specialization to enhance thinking within their field; yet suffering is so uniquely human that to crisply define it with a sociological, neuroscience, or yogic perspective does not seem to be enough. Being in the lives of those with eating disorders asks me to stand in the chasm of unknowing. Philosopher Michel Foucault explains the upsurge in popularity of alternative healing as ". . . a sort of muddled resistance to the obligatory medicalization of their bodies and their illness" (Foucault, 1994, p. 155). I want to believe him. I want answers for why people suffer, and are willing to try anything to rid themselves of the agony they experience. As I thought about how I conceptualize yoga for the treatment of eating disorders I realized that I, like so many other researchers and thinkers before me, "had been searching for answers to my questions in terms that made sense to me . . . and that I needed to begin again" (Luebeck in Delamont, 2002, p. 117). The answers that exist may not reflect the understanding of those who are in front of me, so I listen to their requests and as we think through the body, I watch their embodied expressions with great curiosity and a measure of great care.

Understanding when I rely on one conceptualization of yoga and when I rely on another is a significant component, or at least a start, of bringing mindfulness to the use of yoga as a treatment for individuals with eating disorders. Despite the muddled conceptualization of yoga as therapy for individuals with eating disorders, I believe that yoga is a worthwhile addition to the curriculum. Yoga emphasizes the importance that each individual actively engages in self care, which is a way in which some individuals can reclaim a positive sense of self. The inclusion of yoga can balance the diagnostic and medication that is often essential to healing, with a respect for the body's own healing potential and wisdom (Douglass & Tiwari, 2006). Researchers have proven that yoga reduces cortisol levels, resulting in better health and clearer thinking. Perhaps most importantly, yoga has no answers, but is a method of inquiry. Thinking through the body may help the individual stay grounded in the present moment, and listen to the body, even when what needs to be heard is deeply disconsolate. Yoga's philosophy reminds me that I do not need to solve every conflict, but to create a context, a holding container, in which conflicting ideas, positions, and people are invited to play, to not know, and to imagine new ways of being together in the world.

# REFERENCES

Agte, V. V., & Chiplonkar, S. A. (2008). Sudarshan Kriya Yoga for improving antioxidant status and reducing anxiety in adults. *Alternative & Complementary Therapies, 14*(2), 96–100.

Alter, J. (2009). Yoga in Asia-Mimetic history: Problems in the location of secret knowledge. *Comparative Studies of South Asia, Africa and the Middle East, 29,* 213–229.

Babu, K. S., Burton, H., Chu, M., Cisek, P., Debowy, D., Diamond, M., . . .Yoshioka, T. (2002). *The somatosensory system: Deciphering the brain's own body image* (ed. R. Nelson). New York, NY: CRC Press.

Boudette, R. (2006). Question & answer: Yoga in the treatment of disordered eating and body image disturbance: how can the practice of yoga be helpful in recovery from an eating disorder? *Eating Disorders, 14,* 167–170.

Bourdieu, P., & Passeron, J.-C. (2000). *Reproduction in education, society and culture* (2nd ed.). London, UK: Sage.

Brown, R. P., & Gerbarg, P. L. (2005). Sudarshan kriya yogic breathing in the treatment of stress, anxiety, and depression: Part II clinical applications and guidelines. *Journal of Alternative & Complementary Medicine, 11,* 711–717.

Bundy, A., Lane, S., & Murray, E. (2002). *Sensory integration theory and practice.* Philadelphia, PA: F. A. Davis.

Carlson, L. E., Speca, M., Patel, K. D., & Goodey, E. (2004). Mindfulness-based stress reduction in relation to quality of life, mood, symptoms of stress and levels of cortisol, dehydroepiandrosterone sulfate (DHEAS) and melatonin in breast and prostate cancer outpatients. *Psychoneuroendocrinology, 29,* 448–474.

da Silva, T. L., Ravindran, L. N., & Ravindran, A. V. (2009). Yoga in the treatment of mood and anxiety disorders: A review. *Asian Journal of Psychiatry, 2*(1), 6–16.

Dalal, A. S. (2001a). *A greater psychology: An introduction to Sri Aurobindo's psychological thought.* New York:, NY Jeremy Tarcher/ Putnam Press.

Dalal, A. S. (2001b). *Psychology, mental health and yoga* (2nd ed.). Pondicherry, India: Sri Aurobindo Ahram Press

Damasio, A. (1999). *The feeling of what happens.* New York, NY: Hartcourt, Brace.

Delamont, S. (2002). *Fieldwork in educational settings: Methods pitfalls and perspectives* (2nd ed.). New York, NY: Routledge.

Desikachar, T., & Cravens, R. (1998). *Health, healing and beyond: Yoga and the living tradition of Krishnamacharya.* New York, NY: Aperture Foundation.

Douglass, L. (2009). Yoga as an intervention for eating disorders: Does it help? *Eating Disorders, 17,* 126–139.

Douglass, L., & Tiwari, S. (2006). Integrating Yoga cikitsa in the West: Challenges and future directions *International journal of Yoga Therapy, 16,* 21–32.

Foucault, M. (1994). *Power.* New York, NY: The New York Press.

Goldberg, C. (2001). Cognitive processes in panic disorder: An extension of current models. *Psychological Reports, 88,* 139–159.

Granath, J., Ingvarsson, S., von Thiele, U., & Lundberg, U. (2006). Stress management: a randomized study of cognitive behavioural therapy and yoga. *Cognitive Behaviour Therapy, 35,* 3–10.

Hoyez, A.-C. C. (2007). The "world of yoga": The production and reproduction of therapeutic landscapes. *Social Science & Medicine, 65*(1), 112–124.

Kelly, P., & Colquhoun, D. (2003). Governing the stressed self: Teacher "health and well-being" and "effective schools." *Discourse: Studies in the Cultural Politics of Education, 24,* 191–205.

Kelly, P., & Colquhoun, D. (2005). The professionalization of stress management: Health and well-being as a professional duty of care? *Critical Public Health, 15,* 135–145.

Krishnamurti, J. (2003). *Beginnings of learning* (3rd ed.). London, UK: Phoenix.

Krishnananda, S. (2009). *Lessons of the Upanishads.* [Electronic Version] Retrieved from http://www.swami-krishnananda.org/upanishad/upan_pub.html

Lakoff, G., & Johnson, M. (1999). *Philosophy in the flesh: The embodied mind and its challenges to Western thought.* New York, NY: Basic Books.

Lavey, R., Sherman, T., Mueser, K., Osbourne, D., Currier, M., & Wolfe, R. (2005). The effects of Yoga on mood on psychiatric inpatients. *Psychiatric Rehabilitation Journal, 28,* 399–402.

McIver, S., O'Halloran, P., & McGartland, M. (2009). Yoga as a treatment for binge eating disorder: A preliminary study. *Complementary Therapies in Medicine, 17,* 196–202.

Meuret, A. E., Ritz, T., Wilhelm, F. H., & Roth, W. T. (2005). Voluntary hyperventilation in the treatment of panic disorder—Functions of hyperventilation, their implications for breathing training, and recommendations for standardization. *Clinical Psychology Review, 25,* 285–306.

Michalsen, A., Grossman, P., Acil, A., Langhorst, J., Ludtke, R., Esch, T. . . .Dobox, G. J. (2005). Rapid stress reduction and anxiolysis among distressed women as a consequence of a three-month intensive yoga program. *Medical Science Monitor, 11,* CR555–561.

Mitchell, K. S., Mazzeo, S. E., Rausch, S. M., & Cooke, K. L. (2007). Innovative interventions for disordered eating: Evaluating dissonance-based and yoga interventions. *The International Journal of Eating Disorders, 40,* 120–128.

Ogden, P., Minton, K., & Pain, C. (2006). *Trauma and the body: A sensorimotor approach to psychotherapy.* New York, NY: W. W. Norton & Company.

Peters, M., Bowman, W., Shusterman, R., Markula, P., Mans, M., Walsh, D., . . . Garioian, C. (2004). *Knowing bodies, moving minds: Towards an embodied teaching and learning* (Vol. 3). Boston, MA: Klumer Academic Publishers.

Radakrishna, S. (1998). *Indian philosophy* (Vol. 2). Delhi, India: Oxford Press.

Rothschild, B. (2000). *The body remembers: The psychophysiology of trauma and trauma treatment.* New York, NY: W. W. Norton & Company.

Salmon, P., Lush, E., Jablonski, M., & Sephton, S. E. (2009). Yoga and mindfulness: Clinical aspects of an ancient mind/body practice. *Cognitive and Behavioral Practice, 16*(1), 59–72.

Sankaracharya, S., Suresvaracharya, S., & Vidyaranya, S. (1993). *The Taittiriya Upanishad* (A. M. Sastry, Trans.). Madras, India: Samata Books.

Satchidananda, S. (2003). *The Yoga sutras of Patanjali* (9th ed.). Buckingham, VA: Integral Yoga Publications.

Scime, M., & Cook-Cottone, C. (2008). Primary prevention of eating disorders: A consctructivst integration of mind and body strategies. *International Journal of Eating Disorders 41,* 134–142.

Scime, M., Cook-Cottone, C., Kane, L., & Watson, T. (2006). Group prevention of eating disorders with fifth-grade females: Impact on body dissatisfaction, drive for thinness, and media influence. *Eating Disorders, 14,* 143–155.

Seid, R., Wooley, O. W., Rothblum, E., Perlick, D., Silverstein, B., Wolf, N., . . . Striegel-Moore, R. (1994). *Feminist perspectives on eating disorders.* New York, NY: The Guilford Press.

Shannahoff-Khalsa, D. S. (2004). An introduction to Kundalini yoga meditation techniques that are specific for the treatment of psychiatric disorders. *Journal of Alternative and Complementary Medicine, 10*(1), 91–101.

Shapiro, S. B. (1999). *Pedagogy and the politics of the body: A critical praxis* (Vol. 16). New York, NY: Garland Publishing.

Sharma, V. K., Das, S., Mondal, S., Goswami, U., & Gandhi, A. (2006). Effect of Sahaj Yoga on neuro-cognitive functions in patients suffering from major depression. *Indian Journal of Physiology and Pharmacology, 50,* 375–383.

Shusterman, R. (2006). Thinking through the body, educating for the humanities: A pleas for somaesthics. *Journal of Aesthetic Education, 40*(1), 1–21.

Siegel, D. (2010). *Mindsight: The new science of personal transformation.* New York, NY: Bantam Books.

Smith, C., Hancock, H., Blake-Mortimer, J., & Eckert, K. (2007). A randomised comparative trial of yoga and relaxation to reduce stress and anxiety. *Complementary Therapies in Medicine, 15*(2), 77–83.

Wald, J., & Taylor, S. (2008). Responses to interoceptive exposure in people with Posttraumatic Stress Disorder (PTSD): A preliminary analysis of induced anxiety reactions and trauma memories and their relationship to anxiety sensitivity and PTSD symptom severity. *Cognitive Behaviour Therapy, 37,* 90–100.

West, J., Otte, C., Geher, K., Johnson, J., & Mohr, D. C. (2004). Effects of Hatha yoga and African dance on perceived stress, affect, and salivary cortisol. *Annals of Behavioral Medicine, 28,* 114–118.

Zull, J., Cozolino, L., Sprokay, S., Perry, B., Ross, C., Wolfe, P., . . . Taylor, K. (2006). *The neuroscience of adult learning.* San Francisco, CA: Jossey Bass.

# Features

# Using Mindful Eating to Treat Food Restriction: A Case Study

SUSAN ALBERS

*Private practice, Wooster, Ohio, USA*

*This case study describes the application of the principles of mindful eating to the treatment of a case of anorexia nervosa. While many clinicians currently use mindful eating in their treatment of binge eating disorder and bulimia, it also may benefit clients who restrict. The client in this case study is a 19-year-old college student with a BMI of 17.9 and daily restriction of approximately 900–1000 calories who exercises 1 hour daily. Over 15 sessions, she was introduced to the principle of mindful eating. There was an overall decline in restriction, her BMI raised to 19.5, and her caloric intake increased to approximately 1,500–2,000.*

Therapists have begun investigating the utility of "mindfulness" in treating a number of clinical disorders (Baer, 2003; Linehan, Schmidt, Craft, Kanter, & Comtois, 1999; Ludwig & Kabat-Zinn, 2008; Proulx, 2003; Shapiro, Schwartz, & Bonner, 1998; Teasdale, 2004), particularly its effectiveness as a component of eating disorder treatments (Proulx, 2008; Safer, Telch, & Agras, 2001a; Wisniewski & Kelly, 2003). Mindfulness is generally defined as intentionally drawing one's awareness and attention to the present moment in a nonjudgmental and accepting way (Kabat-Zinn, 1990; Tapper, Shaw, Ilsley, Hill, Bond, & Moore, 2009). It includes bringing the qualities of awareness, openness, nonjudgment, accepting, nonreactivity, and compassion in the present moment to all experiences, both pleasant and unpleasant (Kabat-Zinn, 1990).

Mindfulness, as applied to eating, has been defined as, "a nonjudgmental awareness of physical and emotional sensations associated with eating"

(Framson et al., 2009, p. 1439). It is being present with internal emotions, thoughts, and sensations as well as the external sensations associated with eating. This includes being attentive and in-the-moment with the sensation of taste, awareness of satiety cues, cognition, and emotions associated with eating (Andersen, 2007).

While mindful eating approaches are currently used to treat binge eating disorder (Baer, Fischer, & Huss, 2005; Kristeller & Hallett, 1999; Proulx, 2008; Telch, Agras, & Linehan, 2001), bulimia (Safer, Telch, & Agras, 2001a; Safer, Telch, & Agras, 2001b), and weight management (Framson et al., 2009; Tapper et al. 2009), there is a growing interest in adapting it for use with clients who restrict their food intake (Andersen, 2007; Heffner & Eifert, 2004; Rawal, Enayati, Williams, & Park, 2009; Wisniewski & Kelly, 2003).

Several therapies have already incorporated mindful eating into their approaches such as Acceptance and Commitment Therapy (ACT; Hayes & Smith, 2005), Dialectical Behavioral Therapy (DBT; Linehan, 1993), and Mindfulness Based Eating Awareness Training (MB-EAT; Kristeller & Hallett, 1999). At the core of these approaches, is the teaching of self awareness, affect regulation, acceptance, and nonjudgment.

Mindfulness is thought to help emotional regulation and adaptive functioning (Lykins & Baer, 2009). Individuals with anorexia have been found to have deficits in affect regulation skills and emotional awareness (Gilboa-Schechtman, Avnon, & Jeczmien, 2006, Wisniewski & Kelly, 2003). Thus, the principles of mindful eating may hold therapeutic benefits because they target affect regulation skills.

Mindful eating is the process of being more aware of and less reactive to distressing thoughts about food, body and shape, and overwhelming emotions about food. The clinical features of anorexia that cause emotional dysregulation are fear of food, irrational fear of fatness, intensive drive for thinness, body image distortion, and excessive reliance on weight and shape for self-esteem. Instead of dwelling and ruminating on eating disordered thoughts, mindfulness encourages changing the way one relates to these distressing thought patterns, replacing restriction with healthier, adaptive coping skills.

CBT has generally been considered the first choice in treatment for eating disorders. However, there is a need for more effective treatments due to the drop out rates (Sly, 2009) and relapse (Carter, Blackmor, Sutandar-Pinnock, & Woodside, 2004; Federici & Kaplan, 2008). Mindfulness based treatment may be a viable option due to its success with other clinical disorders. This case study presents an example of how mindfulness was incorporated into the individual treatment of a woman with a diagnosis of anorexia nervosa.

## CASE REPORT

The client was a 19-year-old, single, Caucasian female with a history of food restriction and anxiety. She was a freshman at a small private college. Prior to this counseling, she had completely only three therapy sessions in high school. Her presenting problem at the time of her initial counseling was anxiety over her performance in athletic events. She refused to go back to counseling because she was "turned off" by the counselor's approach to her problems. Her perception of past counseling suggested that she may be a candidate for a different approach than cognitive behavioral therapy. The specific details of this client have been altered to conceal her identity.

No one had identified the client's issues during high school despite the client's frequent dieting and weight loss. She indicated feeling that she needed to lose weight in high school to improve her sports performance and in response to critical comments by her coach. The client did not have any concurrent medical problems and was not taking any kind of medication prior to or during treatment.

The client was referred to therapy by the college health center when the client expressed concern that her menstruation cycle had stopped/been irregular. The physician suspected the presence of an eating disorder. The transition to college had been difficult for this client. She struggled with the intensity of the academic workload and she had not been granted playing time on her team sport. She had lost approximately 10 pounds over a month. In addition, her mother expressed mild concern about her weight loss. However, this concern was not unequivocal. Her mother also expressed envy about her weight loss.

The client had become very focused on food and expressed a number of eating disordered thoughts during the initial session (i.e., "If I eat a cookie, I'll gain two pounds."). Her eating habits had become rigid and repetitive. She ate the same foods every day and had cut out meat and some dairy. As her weight dropped, she began to isolate and refuse dinner invitations from friends.

## TREATMENT

The treatment involved 15 individual sessions that focused on integrating mindful eating skills into each session. The length of the treatment was based on real world constraints such as length of her semester, session coverage and remittance of symptoms.

The type of treatment that would be conducted was discussed when the therapist reviewed the informed consent. This included explaining the research linked to mindful eating, rationale, limitations, and the other forms of treatments available. She was free to decline this type of treatment if she wished.

During the initial session, the client was asked to keep a mindful eating journal. This is a record of food intake as well as her thoughts, feelings and perception of her body/satiety cues at each meal. This was intended to help raise her awareness of the connection between her thoughts, feelings and actions.

The treatment was adapted from mindful eating exercises from a variety of texts on mindfulness (Albers, 2003; Albers, 2008; Heffner & Eifert, 2004; Kabat-Zinn, 1990; Hayes & Smith, 2005). Key components included: a) mindful eating: tasting food; b) mindfulness of hunger; c) being in-the-moment; d) letting go; e) acceptance; and, f) compassion and nonjudgment.

## MINDFUL EATING: TASTING FOOD

After the intake, the initial session began with a brief introduction to mindful eating. The format was adapted from a classic mindful eating exercise (Kabat-Zinn, 1990; Proulx, 2008). The therapist chose a piece of chocolate for the exercise. It was intentionally chosen because the client labeled "junk food" and "candy" as fear foods. She acknowledged that eating chocolate would raise her anxiety. The therapist read the script adapted from Albers (2008, p. 76):

*Instructions: Get into a comfortable position. Relax and close your eyes. Use all of your senses.*

*Take one piece of chocolate in your hand. Observe the shape and color. As you unwrap it, listen to the crinkle of the foil or wrapper. Touch it and feel the texture between your fingertips as you pick it up. Silently describe the chocolate to yourself. Notice the shape. Roll it around in your hands. Bring the chocolate up to your nose and inhale deeply. Take a few deep breaths in and out. Be aware of what is happening in your mind. Let the thoughts come and go. Place the chocolate in your mouth. As you begin to chew, observe the flavor. The richness. The sweetness. Experience the taste. Notice as the texture changes and molds to your tongue and breaks down in your mouth. Roll the chocolate against the roof of your mouth. Don't try to push away any emotions that pop into your mind as you eat the chocolate. Just notice the thoughts. Let them float past you. Listen to the sound of your jaw chewing. Feel the sensation as the chocolate slides down your throat. Imagine the piece of chocolate in your stomach. Open your eyes.*

The client expressed anxiety in simply holding the piece of chocolate in her hand. It took her several minutes to put the chocolate in her mouth. The therapist asked the client to describe the chocolate and to talk about the feelings and thoughts that came into her mind as she was eating the chocolate. According to the client, the feelings that it aroused included not only fear, but also desire and anxiety. The thoughts associated with these feelings included, "if I eat this chocolate, I will lose control and want more," and, "this food will make me fat." Making her aware of the automatic thoughts that came to mind when she saw and interacted with her fear foods helped her to respond more mindfully to them. Rather than obeying, believing, or becoming overwhelmed by her thoughts, she labeled them as, "just thoughts." She was encouraged to allow and embrace discomfort rather than avoid it. By directly experiencing the anxiety related to contact with fear food, she became habituated to her inner experience. In so doing, she learned to tolerate it. By the end of counseling, she had begun accepting dinner invitations and attending social events that served food—instead of avoiding them.

## MINDFULNESS OF HUNGER

Mindful eating is helpful in teaching body awareness. Attending to self and body in an experiential way can improve emotional regulation in people with eating disorders, according to the findings by Rawal et al. (2009).

When initially asked about her sensation of hunger and fullness, the client indicated that she had little awareness of when she was physically hungry and bodily full. She made statements like, "I'm not sure if I am hungry or not," and "I typically don't eat in the morning because I don't think I should be hungry yet." During the session, the therapist asked the client to tune into her hunger in that moment. This included describing the sensations in her body as they were speaking in the present. In other words, the therapist invited her to both become aware of the sensations occurring in her body in-the-moment and connect them to how she was feeling. The client responded that the physical sensation of hunger she experienced in her body felt "hollow" and "scary."

When the client's stomach growled during the session, the client initially denied that it was due to hunger. She stated, "My stomach just makes noises sometimes." However, she admitted being afraid of feeling hungry and talking herself into believing that the noises were not hunger. The therapist would gently acknowledge the client's rumbling stomach when it "made noises" in future sessions and discuss what her body was telling her.

For homework, the client was asked to complete a handout (Albers, 2008, p. 70). It was a worksheet to track her hunger throughout various points in the day. The client rated and recorded her level of hunger on a scale from 1 to 10, with 1 being very hungry and 10 being completely full. The client returned the homework after each session. The worksheet helped to highlight that there were typical, predictable patterns in her hunger. She reported understanding that, "I do get hungry and it is okay to be hungry."

## BEING IN-THE-MOMENT

Mindful being-in-the moment helps clients to be less reactive and avoidant of uncomfortable internal experiences. Food restriction is often a means of diverting attention from overwhelming emotions (Rawal et al., 2009). It is difficult for those with restricting tendencies, particularly when overwhelmed, to be present with intense feelings. Restriction is one way to push away these feelings or numb them out.

In the therapy sessions, the client was taught how to be in-the-moment and present emotionally when experiencing the urge to restrict. Throughout the counseling, the client identified several emotional triggers of eating disordered behavior. For example, seeing her coach increased her anxiety and stress. When she walked into a busy cafeteria, she felt overwhelmed by the number of choices. She felt confused when she received mixed messages from her mother about her weight. Each of these was a strong trigger for her. When she encountered one of these triggers, she was instructed to be still for several minutes and journal about it. Journaling was a tool for the client to be present with her feelings instead of moving automatically into her typical reaction to restrict. The therapist likened the client's immediate response to restrict to a "knee-jerk" reaction. Mindfulness slows down this "knee-jerk" reaction. It creates a moment in time in which the patient may feel distressed without feeling compelled to act on it with restriction.

By nonjudgmentally noticing and being aware of the urge to restrict before acting on it, she could more accurately identify her feelings and respond with more adaptive coping skills. For example, she frequently observed her distressed internal state when seeing her coach. She saw the coach several times a day. In response, the client was taught mindful breathing, a healthier response to anxiety than restriction (Albers, 2003, p. 75). Mindful breathing is simply exhaling and inhaling slowly while counting. The client used mindful breathing to draw awareness to her body instead of her thoughts. It helped her to disengage from eating disordered and stressful cognitions. Rather than ruminating and dwelling on the urge to restrict, she mindfully directed her thoughts to her body to reduce her anxiety behaviorally. In addition, mindful breathing enabled her to relax and get into a mindful state (Kabat-Zinn, 1990).

## LETTING GO

A component of mindfulness is "let go" of thoughts rather than clinging to them (Kabat-Zinn, 1990). Suffering comes from holding onto, ruminating, and believing destructive thoughts to be facts rather than just thoughts. This is a helpful concept for clients with eating disorder. In particular, clients who restrict are reactive to their inner critic and ruled by destructive eating disorder thoughts.

The client's initial goal was to "get rid of her eating disorder voice" and to "make it go away." Instead, the client was taught the notion of acknowledging the presence of her eating disordered thoughts and letting them go. We can neither control our thoughts nor erase them. Struggling against them only adds to the suffering they cause, as was evident by her wish to just not have the thoughts.

The client was introduced to the term of nonattachment. She could have the eating disordered thoughts without becoming too closely involved with them. When experiencing an eating disordered thought, she was instructed to gently acknowledge the presence of them and use visual imagery to distance herself from them. Linehan (1993) described distancing from thoughts to be like placing thoughts in boxes on a conveyor belt and letting them go by without picking them up. The metaphor used with this client was to imagine placing each thought on a balloon and allowing them to fly away, one at time.

After learning the concept, the client returned to the next session with examples of her eating disordered thoughts. She described how she used visual imagery to let them go without reacting or trying to change the thoughts. She reported having thoughts such as, "I shouldn't eat that" or "pizza is bad." She talked about how she imagined placing each eating disordered thought in a balloon and mentally releasing the balloon into the air. She was able to acknowledge, however, that some thoughts were, "more difficult to let go of than others." This called for continued practice. Clients often want to judge their performance. In this instance, the client was encouraged to adopt a nonjudgmental attitude toward learning and practicing these skills—to notice her efforts to use visual imagery without grading her performance.

## ACCEPTANCE

Acceptance is defined as being open and receptive to the reality of whatever one is hearing, thinking, or seeing (Kabat-Zinn, 1990). It is not judging the situation to be good or bad but allowing it to be what it is without trying to change it. The client was taught three aspects of acceptance: acceptance of acceptance of food, hunger, and self/body image.

Acceptance was integral to the client's increase in food intake and tolerance of her hunger. It was okay for the client to not like or be unhappy with the need to increase her calories. However, she was asked to extend a willingness to accept an increase in the quantity and variety of food that she would eat. The therapist helped the client to allow herself to be not only be ambivalent, but also accepting of her body's need for calories. The client, unfortunately, did not have access to a nutritionist to help define this food plan. However, the client was well versed in nutritious foods and calorie content.

The client found herself struggling between allowing herself to experience the sensation of hunger and acting on the desire to want to change it and "make it go away." When mindfully noticing cues of hunger, she referred back to the notion of acceptance, of allowing the sensations to be what they were without attempting to alter them. When the client became aware of herself trying to change her hunger or emotions, she repeated this acceptance mantra to herself, "allow it to be, just as it is" (Albers, 2008).

Finally, the notion of acceptance was used to help address her body image concerns. The client took home a list of acceptance affirmations to repeat to herself. She was also encouraged to practice these affirmations when she was distressed. She also was encouraged to practice them when she was not experiencing emotional dysregulation. Examples of the self-body affirmations include, "I appreciate the body I've been given" and "my body is powerful." In addition, the client was instructed to use acceptance affirmations when she found herself comparing her body to other people's bodies and using body checking to reassure herself of thinness.

## COMPASSION AND NONJUDGMENT

Judgment and self criticism are central features of anorexia and personified in the "eating disorder voice." Individuals with eating disorders tend to be highly perfectionistic and self-critical (Rawal et al., 2009). The client was taught to be mindful by "hearing" the eating disorder voice without agreeing with the content of the statements and to use compassion and nonjudgment. Examples of statements made by the client's eating disorder internal "voice" included, "your thighs are fat," and "you didn't make the team because the coach thought you were too fat."

The goal of this component was to teach compassionate and neutral statements to help respond to the internal critical statements that caused emotional distress. When faced with critical statements, she was instructed to counter them. For example to use neutral and compassionate words like, "that is just my eating disorder talking," "that was a very painful thought," or "your worth is not dependent on your weight."

The client made cue cards to help her bring these thoughts to mind when her inner, critical voice was present. The client reported that it was difficult to "believe" the statements. However, with repeated practice, these words came more naturally without the aid of cue cards. Overall, the client noted that initially she was unaware of how critical her mind was and how judgmental she was of herself and others. The practice of being mindful allowed her to make the judgments conscious and to respond mindfully to the judgments with an open, compassionate mind.

## RESULTS

After learning the principles of mindful eating, there was a decline in restriction, her BMI raised to 19.5 and caloric intake increased to approximately 1,500–2,000. In addition, the client reported an improvement in the quantity and variety of foods that she consumed. This was documented in her food journal. Moreover, she reported an increase in her consumption of her "fear foods" such as pizza, milk, and some meats. The client, overall, observed a decrease in her eating disordered thinking. Specifically, she indicated less ruminating and emotional distress. In the future, the cognitive and behavioral changes could be evaluated by pre-post objective assessment measures. This was not part of the current treatment due to time and lack of availability of these measures. This study is based on the client's self report.

## LIMITATIONS

Mindful eating should be used thoughtfully and by those trained in the concepts. Further research needs to be conducted to evaluate its usefulness with anorexic patients. The client in this study was at a low weight, but she did not present as significantly underweight or medically compromised. Clients who are at a low weight may not be able to cognitively focus on the moment or become overwhelmed by being present with emotionally difficult material. This is an example of just one case which also limits its broad range applicability. Determining its usefulness in larger scale studies and with patients who have chronic issues would be helpful. The client in this study was able to recognize a problem and was at a stage that she was willing to work on the issue. Not all patients may be open to this form of treatment.

It is difficult to determine whether the client would have benefited from any therapy or this particular kind. She responded positively and praised the approach. In particular, she noted that it, "took her feelings and thoughts seriously." The gentleness of the approach seemed to match her personality and needs.

## DISCUSSION

Mindful eating skills may be a helpful approach in treating medically stable clients who are coping with restriction. The approach may assist clients in regulating their affect when confronted with overwhelming and distressing thoughts and feelings in the presence of food or during the act of eating. Further research and observation is needed and would help in understanding the utility of this treatment as well as its underlying mechanisms.

Mindfulness is noted to be compatible with other forms of treatment such as CBT (Baer & Sauer, 2009). Thus, using mindful eating as a component or adjunct to well established treatments maybe a future avenue of research to explore.

## REFERENCES

Albers, S. (2003). *Eating mindfully*. Oakland CA: New Harbinger Publications.

Albers, S. (2008). *Eat, drink & be mindful*. Oakland CA: New Harbinger Publications.

Andersen, A. (2007). Stories I tell my patients: Where are you when you are eating? *Eating Disorders, 15*, 279–280.

Baer, R. A. (2003). Mindfulness training as a clinical intervention: A conceptual and empirical review. *Clinical Psychology Science and Practice, 10*, 125–143.

Baer, R. A., Fischer, S., & Huss, D. B. (2005). Mindfulness-based cognitive therapy applied to binge eating: A case study. *Cognitive and Behavioral Practice, 12*, 351–358.

Baer, R. A., & Sauer, S. (2009). Mindfulness and cognitive behavioral therapy: A commentary on Harrington and Pickles. *Journal of Cognitive Psychotherapy, 23*, 324–332.

Carter, J. C., Blackmor, E., Sutandar-Pinnock, K., & Woodside, D. B. (2004). Relapse in AN: A survival analysis. *Psychological Medicine, 4*, 671–679.

Federici, A., & Kaplan, A. S. (2008). The patient's account of relapse and recovery in anorexia nervosa: A qualitative study. *European Eating Disorders Review, 16*(1), 1–10.

Framson, C., Kristal, A. R., Schenk, J. M., Littman, A. J., Zeliadt, S,. & Benitez, D. (2009). Development and validation of the mindful eating questionnaire. *Journal of the American Dietetic Association, 109*, 1439–1444.

Gilboa-Schechtman, E., Avnon, S. A. & Jeczmien, P. (2006). Emotional processing in eating disorders: Specific impairment or general distress related deficiency? *Depression and Anxiety, 23*, 331–333.

Hayes, S. C., & Smith, S. (2005). *Getting out of your mind and into your life*. Oakland CA: New Harbinger Publications.

Heffner, M., & Eifert, G. H. (2004). *The anorexia workbook: How to accept yourself, heal your suffering, and reclaim your life*. Oakland, CA: New Harbinger.

Kabat-Zinn, J. (1990). *Full catastrophe living*. New York, NY: Bantam Doubleday Dell Publishing Group.

Kristeller, J. L., & Hallett, C. B. (1999). An exploratory study of a meditation-based intervention for binge eating disorder. *Journal of Health Psychology, 4*, 357–363.

Linehan, M. M. (1993). *Skills training manual for treating borderline personality disorder*. New York, NY: The Guilford Press

Linehan, M. M., Schmidt, H., Craft, J. C., Kanter, J., & Comtois, K. A. (1999). Dialectical behavior therapy for patients with borderline personality disorder and drug dependence. *American Journal of Addictions, 8*, 279–292.

Ludwig, D. S., & Kabat-Zinn, J. (2008). Mindfulness in medicine. *Journal of the American Medical Association, 300*, 1350–1352.

Lykins, E. L. B., & Baer, R. A. (2009). Psychological functioning in a sample of long-term practitioners of mindfulness meditation. *Journal of Cognitive Psychotherapy, 23,* 226–241.

Proulx, K. (2003). Integrating mindfulness-based stress reduction. *Holistic Nurse Practice, 17,* 201–208.

Proulx, K. (2008). Experiences of women with bulimia nervosa in a mindfulness-based eating disorder treatment group. *Eating Disorders, 16,* 52–72.

Rawal, A., Enayati, J., Williams, M., & Park, R. (2009). A mindful approach to eating disorders. *Healthcare Counseling & Psychotherapy Journal, 9*(4), 16–20.

Safer D. L., Telch, C. F., & Agras, W. S. (2001a). Dialectical behavior therapy adapted for bulimia: A case report. *International Journal of Eating Disorders, 30,* 101–106.

Safer, D. L., Telch, C. F., & Agras, W. S. (2001b). Dialectical behavior therapy for bulimia nervosa. *American Journal of Psychiatry, 158,* 632–634.

Shapiro, S. L., Schwartz, G. E., & Bonner, G. (1998). Effects of mindfulness-based stress reduction on medical and premedical students. *Journal of Behavioral Medicine, 21,* 581–599.

Sly, R. (2009). What's in a name? Classifying "the dropout" from treatment for anorexia nervosa. *European Eating Disorders Review, 17,* 405–407.

Tapper, K., Shaw, C., Ilsley, J., Hill, A. J., Bond, F. W., & Moore, L. (2009). Exploratory randomised controlled trial of a mindfulness-based weight loss intervention for women. Appetite, *52,* 396–404.

Telch, C. F., Agras, W. S., & Linehan, M. M. (2001). Dialectical behavior therapy for binge eating disorder. *Journal of Consulting and Clinical Psychology, 69,* 1061–1065.

Teasdale, J. D. (2004). Mindfulness-based cognitive therapy. In J. Yiend (Ed.), *Cognition, emotion and psychopathology: Theoretical, empirical and clinical directions* (pp. 270–289). New York, NY: Cambridge University Press.

Wisniewski, L., & Kelly, E. (2003). Can DBT be used to effectively treat eating disorders? *Cognitive and Behavioral Practice, 10,* 131–138.

# Integrating Mindfulness Into the Therapy Hour

ROBIN BOUDETTE

*Counseling and Psychological Services, Princeton University Health Services, Princeton, New Jersey, USA*

## INTRODUCTION

*"If you have the urge to binge, once you are standing at the refrigerator with both doors open, it's too late. You're going in."*

I used to say this to my clients. I believed and understood, through their self reports, that the urge to binge was impossible to resist once they were caught in this magic momentum. In other words, they would reach a point of no return. The unwanted habit was destined to be repeated.

After studying and practicing mindfulness, I no longer hold this view. I have learned that when we are able to slow things down and take a closer look, new choices become visible. Through slowing down *and* observing—moment by moment—a space opens. Within this space, awareness is possible. Awareness, in turn, offers the possibility of choice. The links in the chain of habit can be broken and new behaviors can emerge.

After more than 15 years of specializing in the treatment of disordered eating, I have been surprised by how my studies and practice of mindfulness have changed the way I work as a psychologist. While I continue to understand and think about the roots of disordered eating in the same way, how I practice has evolved. I place emphasis less on education and interpretation and more on mindfulness or nonjudgmental, present moment awareness

The authors thanks Elizabeth Mackenzie and Mary Saraco for their helpful comments in preparing this article.

(Kabat-Zinn, 1990). Increasingly, I direct clients to tune-in to their immediate sensations, thoughts, and emotions. As my emphasis has changed, I have noticed a positive effect on my patients and their relationship to food and eating. My experience has shown me how integrating mindfulness in therapy sessions facilitates the recovery process in both deep and dramatic ways.

## BRINGING MINDFULNESS INTO SESSIONS

Although I have observed firsthand how mindfulness benefits clients, it is still challenging for me to bring mindfulness into sessions. One challenge is my own confidence with applying mindfulness in individual therapy sessions. What one may use or do in a group setting does not readily fit into individual therapy. Even with training, guiding clients in mindfulness has been a step outside my comfort zone. Establishing a personal practice of mindfulness meditation and receiving mindfulness training has helped me to develop both my own awareness and my skills as a therapist. With this development, I have become more confident. It has been a gradual process and I continue to learn more over time.

Another challenge is that many clients come to therapy wanting to talk about, rather than connect with, their bodies and feelings. Many are turned off by the word "mindfulness." By necessity, I have learned to weave mindfulness into the therapy hour in subtle ways that engage the client's curiosity. Once they are interested, I then judiciously offer mindful eating practices and mindfulness-based interventions at a pace I think they can handle.

Disordered eating is grounded in disconnection from the body, appetite, feelings, the present moment, other people, and one's own inner wisdom. Clients often come to therapy avoiding connection to their own experiences. I look for openings in the therapy hour where I can seamlessly introduce connecting to present experience in non-threatening ways. For example, when a client says, "I don't know where to begin," or "I don't know what to say," or "I forgot what I was saying," I suggest that they take a moment to become aware. I begin with: "Let's pause." I say: "Sit for a moment and notice what's happening right now. For the moment, you don't need to talk. Just notice. Turn your attention to what's happening. What sensations are here right now? What thoughts are going through your mind? What emotions are present?" This is the first step in shifting away from thinking about the problem and moving toward feeling and being in the present moment. As the content of the problem falls into the background, I guide clients in turning toward their experience and ask them to observe and note whatever arises.

## OBSERVING AND NOTING

Observing and noting is neither easy nor obvious for clients whose habit is to be disconnected from themselves and others. I often guide clients through the process of observing and noting by introducing the "Triangle of Awareness" (McCown, Reibel & Micozzzi, 2010). The three points of the triangle are bodily sensations, thoughts, and emotions. I describe awareness as a spotlight that moves along the points of the triangle illuminating—without judgment—whatever arises. Using the "Triangle of Awareness," clients' bodily sensations, thoughts, and emotions become anchors into the present moment. This enables clients to feel and label their direct experience as well as develop the capacity to observe without judgment. Indeed, I encourage them to be curious rather than critical. Gradually, clients learn to distinguish different aspects of direct experience: "This is burning in the stomach . . . there are those self-critical thoughts . . . this is anxiety."

For those clients who report too much mental restlessness to focus their attention, speaking aloud can be helpful. I often begin by demonstrating: "I am aware of tension in my neck . . . I am aware of feeling tired . . . I am aware of thoughts about this exercise." Subsequently, I will ask them to try it for themselves—to observe and note aloud the bodily sensations, thoughts, and emotions they are experiencing while sitting with me in the session. This simple step of pausing to notice what is happening enables clients to disengage from automatic habit patterns and be with their immediate experience. The noting that follows helps to create an observing self, separate from the changing internal experience. By observing, noting, and accepting passing internal experiences, clients learn to regulate their emotions without engaging in negative behaviors. Mindfulness can become an alternative to acting on impulses and cravings.

For Linda, a 35-year-old woman with a long history of binge eating disorder and a co-existing anxiety disorder, this technique led to a turning point in therapy. She was ambivalent about engaging in therapy and working with me as well as connecting to her body and her feelings. She would begin every session with "I don't know where to begin." Each time, I would direct her to attend to her inner experience. This introduced her to a safe way to move toward, rather than away from, her inner world. Linda could observe the physical sensations of avoidance such as the tightening in her stomach and tension in her throat. Simultaneously she could notice her feelings of fear and her thoughts about wanting a different outcome. The more she was able to pause and observe her experiences in sessions, the more she was able to do so outside of sessions. Gradually, her work in therapy enabled her to tolerate her bodily sensations, feelings, and thoughts outside of therapy. She no longer needed to turn to binge eating to avoid her present experience. She became more resilient and less reliant on avoidance as a defense.

## MINDFUL EATING IN THE THERAPY SESSION

Eating with clients in sessions has traditionally been the role of the nutritionist. While I have often used the classic mindfulness practice, "The Raisin Exercise" in sessions with good results, I have been cautious about experimenting with other in-session eating practices. Through Jean Kristeller's Mindfulness-Based Eating Awareness Training (MB-EAT) Program, however, I discovered the many benefits of engaging in mindful eating with clients (Kristeller, 2009). Now, I regularly integrate mindful eating interventions in individual sessions.

"The Raisin Exercise" (Segal, Williams & Teasdale, 2002) involves giving a client a raisin and instructing him or her to experience the raisin through all the senses: sight, smell, touch, even sound, and finally, taste. Often, clients find this exercise frustrating. Sometimes they find it confusing. Regardless, almost always, in my experience, processing the experience facilitates awareness.

Questions to explore include: "What did you notice? How is this different from the way you would usually eat a raisin? What might be different if you ate a meal like this?" By slowing down and taking a closer look, they identify aspects of the eating experience which they typically avoid, such as feeling frustrated, wanting to eat fast, and judging thoughts that occur while eating. I model an attitude of interest and curiosity—observation without evaluation. As a result, clients learn a new way of being with unwanted aspects of the experience. In addition, by doing this activity *in the session,* the client remembers what it *feels like* to eat mindfully. One client's report summarizes a common response to this exercise: "I was thinking the exercise was ridiculous. But then two days later, I would be eating something and I would think, 'This is a really interesting texture,' or 'This smells good.' It made me think about what I eat and how I eat. Now I catch myself and say, 'I can just enjoy this.' I'm being kinder to myself."

The MB-EAT program is filled with multiple mindful eating experiences designed to help clients connect with various aspects of eating such as hunger, fullness and taste satiety. One exercise I found easily transferable to individual therapy sessions is what Kristeller calls, *eating like a gourmet*. In all aspects of disordered eating, our clients are disconnected from the pleasure of the eating experience. *Eating like a gourmet* is, essentially, savoring the tastes of food while eating. I encourage clients to not only notice, but also rate the degree of pleasure in each bite. Using the "Taste Satiety Scale" scale, I ask them to explore: "Is the flavor there? How good is it?" Five bites later, I ask, "How does it taste now?" When they are able to connect with their direct experience, they often notice that the taste is not what they expected and changes over time.

I used this intervention with a client struggling with emotional overeating. She brought in her favorite comfort food, ice cream. As I guided us in eating mindfully together, she began to cry. She noted that the ice cream lost its taste, yet she wanted more. When we explored further, she connected with feelings of loneliness. She wanted the ice cream to block out the loneliness. In that moment, she directly experienced how the ice cream briefly disconnected her from loneliness, but did not eradicate it. This awareness was an important new insight for her. The felt experience of this deeper understanding would help her to behave differently in the future. Feeling the loneliness, without needing to block it out, was the next challenge in our work together.

## MINDFULNESS MEDITATION

Once clients are somewhat comfortable with the mindfulness approach, I introduce the formal practice of mindfulness meditation which involves the process of paying attention to present moment experience with an accepting attitude and gently coming back to begin again when the mind wanders. The formal practice of mindfulness enhances self-monitoring, fosters an observing self and cultivates the self- awareness required for making more authentic and conscious choices. I explain to clients that mindfulness meditation is the foundation for deepening mindful responses and can help to interrupt the links in the chain of destructive patterns. With practice, they find that experiences and insights arising during meditation sessions are often seeds that grow into coping skills for tolerating strong urges and letting go of triggering thoughts that fuel disordered eating.

Since establishing a regular meditation practice can be challenging, I often begin therapy sessions by presenting different short meditations to help the client connect with their direct experience and develop some comfort with these practices. Some clients relate more to mindfulness of sounds. Others are drawn to mindfulness of breath. While some clients need more focus and may count the breath, others do better with a more open approach. This preparation and experimentation is critical since most clients initially feel confused and frustrated. Tailoring and adapting meditation practices individually helps clients learn the techniques, gives them a positive experience, and motivates them to practice outside of sessions. Once they are able to practice independently, I recommend or record audio downloads for them to use between sessions. Guided instructions for a variety of mindful meditations can easily be found on the Internet. These will support clients in practicing at home. I often make recordings that can be individualized to clients' needs, and my voice can offer a calming influence and serve as a transitional object.

During the practice of mindfulness meditation when uncomfortable physical sensations, boredom, and restlessness arise, clients are instructed to observe these experiences without evaluating them. Through this practice, clients develop an observing self, a place from which it is possible to witness rather than react to internal experience. They are able to see clearly how thoughts, sensations, and emotions—both pleasant and unpleasant—arise automatically, stay for a time, and pass, like clouds moving through the sky. To reinforce the skill of observing and accepting, I use the image of a mountain (Kabat-Zinn, 1990). As night turns into day, as the weather changes, and the seasons pass, the essence of the mountain remains the same. The ability to be receptive rather than reactive then transfers to challenges with strong emotions and urges. I have clients who have been able to successfully use their mindfulness skills—observing and accepting the changing constellation of sensations, thoughts and emotions associated with cravings—to refrain from binging and purging. Through practice and repetition, they develop the emotional resilience required to witness without acting and allow the urges to pass.

## LEARNING TO START OVER IN THE PRESENT MOMENT

Mindfulness meditation also assists in dealing with thoughts that trigger disordered eating behaviors. Diet mentality says, "Eat today, begin the diet (or recovery) tomorrow." This thought becomes the hook that pulls clients from the reality of the moment and fuels the binge. One of the most compelling experiences in the recovery process can be to interrupt this thought pattern by learning to "start over" (Moffitt, 2007).

Clients can decrease the intensity and frequency of binges by learning to start over in the present moment. This concept might be easy to discuss, but using it while at the precipice of a binge is not. The act of starting over is practiced repeatedly in mindfulness meditation. When the mind is constantly wandering, the instruction is to notice that it has wandered and then to re-direct the attention back to the object of awareness and begin again. Sometimes the entire meditation is noticing that the mind has wandered, bringing it back and starting over. This willingness to notice the process of thinking, let go of the thought stream, and start over is training for stepping out of habit patterns and starting over in this moment, not some other moment in the future. Rather than believing that thought patterns are too difficult to overcome, we can experience thoughts as passing events in the mind. I now tell my patients, "The best predictor of future behavior is past behavior so what we do now predicts what we will do tomorrow. When trying to change a behavior pattern, it's critical to learn to begin again in this present moment. With the skill of mindfulness, at any point you can remember your intention, catch the impulse and make a different choice. It's never too late to start over."

These are some ways mindfulness can be integrated, subtly or directly, into the therapy hour. These interventions may sound simple, but they are powerful. The act of mindfulness cannot be explained; it must be experienced. The mindfulness approach teaches clients to observe, note, and feel what's happening in the present, aside from the thinking mind, with an attitude of curiosity and acceptance. From this open and non-reactive state, they are more aware and can make more conscious, intentional, and healthy choices. It should be noted that the therapists' ability to lead this journey will be greatly enhanced by their own experience with mindfulness. In fact, it is probably best to establish a regular meditation practice before attempting to teach mindfulness to clients. In the same way that personal therapy supports an understanding of the therapeutic process, practicing mindfulness informs the therapist. Mindfulness is deceiving in that it seems quite simple but actual practice is both challenging and dynamic. Knowing this through experience is critical in relaying mindfulness to clients.

## CONCLUSION

My own venture into the study and practice of mindfulness has been profoundly rewarding and transformative both professionally and personally. The benefits of mindfulness on clinical skills and wellbeing of the therapist have been well-documented (Fulton, 2005; Shapiro, Astin, Bishop, & Cordova 2005). I feel more present and less reactive. I feel an expanded capacity to hold emotions that arise in sessions and have experienced the effectiveness of sitting with, rather than interpreting therapeutic material. I am more aware of my own reactions, avoidance tendencies and habitual patterns that interfere with therapeutic presence. I feel a sense of optimism about the possibilities of each new moment. This is especially important in working with eating disorders, which can be prolonged or even fatal.

In addition, training in mindfulness has offered me new ways of self care. Mindfulness training programs are often a blend of teachings, mindfulness practices, and periods of silence. In contrast to consecutive hours of grueling intellectual, didactic presentations, such trainings are rejuvenating and life enhancing. This model is one that we can take home, embrace to feed the soul, and to prevent burn out. Another benefit is exposure to mindfulness meditation teachers, whose wisdom is grounded in their own experience. Those with and without training in psychology have much to teach us about the nature of the mind. I leave trainings feeling fed, satiated with a sense of gratitude and appreciation for the work that I do. I feel a sense of connection and meaning that extends beyond the therapy hour.

# REFERENCES

Fulton, P. (2005). Mindfulness as clinical training. In C. Germer, R. Siegel, & P. Fulton (Eds.), *Mindfulness and psychotherapy* (pp. 55–72). New York, NY: Guilford Press.

Kabat-Zinn, J. (1990). *Full catastrophe living: Using the wisdom of your body and mind to face stress, pain, and illness.* New York, NY: Dell Publishing.

Kristeller, J. L. (2009). *Omega Institute: Mindfulness-based eating awareness training.* New York, NY: Rhinebeck.

McCown, D., Reiber, D., & Micozzi, M. (2010). *Teaching mindfulness.* New York, NY: Springer.

Moffitt, P. (2007). Starting over. *Yoga Journal, Feb,* 89–91, 140–144.

Segal, Z., Williams, M., & Teasdale, J. (2002). *Mindfulness-based cognitive therapy for depression.* New York, NY: Guilford Press.

Shapiro, S., Astin, J., Bishop, S., & Cordova, M. (2005). Mindfulness-based stress reduction and health care professionals: Results from a randomized controlled trial. *International Journal of Stress Management, 12,* 164–176.

# Index

Note: references to Tables, Figures and Illustrations are in bold